"A TRIBUTE THE MAGIC OF THE MUSE AND THE GRACE OF VERSE AND KNOWLEDGE"

By

JEANETTE CABALLERO

THE MUSE (MOUSAI) IS THE ORIGINAL INSPIRATION FOR POETS. IT'S THE SOURCE OF KNOWLEDGE AND WISDOM OF RELIGIOUS HYMNS. A MYSTERIOUS FOUNTAIN THAT EMANATES AS A SACRED GIFT TO LIGHT OUR WAY.

IN TIME, WE LEARN MANY THINGS, AND FROM BOOKS, WE HEAR THE DISTANT VOICES OF OUR ANCESTORS AND INHERIT THE SPIRITUAL LIFE FROM THE GREATEST OF OUR RACE.

Table of Contents

Secret Wisdom Of Ancient Verses
Part Two
"The Magic Of The Muse"

INTRODUCTION

Beware of the man of one book.
CAVE AB HOMINE UNIUS LIBRI. (St. Thomas Aquinas 1227-1274)

"The natural desire of good men is knowledge" Leonardo DaVinci.

This is a collection of pieces from a large number of works with a mixture of words from holy books, ancient philosophers, poets, and sages from all ages. From known and unknown writers, when known, I have indicated the author of each piece. This collection, as it stands, is disjointed and fragmentary. Some ambiguous words or obsolete expressions might not be identical to the originals to make them short and simple. These are bits and pieces of the great and fruitful intellectual and humanitarian heritage of some of our great ancestors. These writings contain philosophy from around the globe. To remember the gifts and sacrifices from sages, prophets, poets and writers of all ages that keep creation's flame burning with charity and hope.

"As long as the dark foundation of our nature, grim in its all-encompassing egoism, mad in its drive to make that egoism reality, to devour everything and define everything by itself, as long as that foundation is visible, as long as this truly original sin exists within us, there is no logical answer to our existence. 'Petrarch'

With literature, isolation becomes your freedom and delight. Literature in a good mind excites the love of goodness and dissipates or at least diminishes the fear of death. Old books are best because rarely anyone did or wrote anything which was regarded with admiration while he still lived. Only when the ashes of a whole generation have been consigned to the funeral Urn do men pass unbiased judgment, free from jealousy. So, the opinion should be received with equanimity if they are just; if unjust, we must appeal to the unprejudiced judges of posterity."
'Vladimir Solovyov'

"Those who the right course would follow, know well each ANCIENT; his character, his fable and subject. Scope well each page: religion, country and genius of his age: Be civil, never criticize. May Homer's work be your study and delight. Read by day and meditate by night; form your judgment, then bring your best out. Trace the muses upward to their spring; still with itself compared, his text peruse; and let your comment be the Mantuan Muse. Learn to esteem ancient rules; to copy Nature is to copy them." 'Alexander Pope'

PART ONE

There are more things in heaven and earth, Horatio, than are dreamt of in your Philosophy. But come...

'Hamlet, Act 1'

"THE MASONIC HYMN"

A very ancient poem from a modern copy, popular amongst the poor
'Brethren of the mystic tie'

Come all you freemasons that dwell around the globe,
That wear the badge of innocence, I mean the royal robe,
Which Noah he did wear when in the ark he stood,
When the world was destroyed by a deluging flood.

Noah, he was virtuous, in the sight of the Lord,
He loved a freemason that kept the secret word;
For he built the ark, and he planted the first vine,
Now his soul is in heaven like an angel doth shine.

Once, I was blind and could not see the light,
Then, up to Jerusalem, I took my flight,
I was led by the evangelist through a wilderness of care,
You may see by the sign and the badge that I wear.

On the 13th rose the Ark; let us join hand in hand,
For the Lord spoke to Moses by water and by land,
Unto the pleasant river where by Eden did run,
And Eve tempted Adam by the serpent sin.

When I think of Moses, it makes me blush,
All on Mount Horeb, where I saw the burning bush;
My shoes I'll throw off, and my staff I'll cast away,
 And I'll wander like a pilgrim unto my dying day.

When I think of Aaron, it makes me to weep,
Likewise of the Virgin Mary who lay at our Saviour's feet;
'Twas in the garden of Gethsemane where he had the bloody sweat;
Repent, my dearest brethren, before it is too late.

I thought I saw twelve dazzling lights, which put me in a surprise,
And gazing all around me, I heard a dismal noise;
The serpent passed by me, which fell unto the ground,
With great joy and comfort, the secret word I found.

Some say it is lost, but surely it is found,
And so is our Saviour; it is known to all around;
Search all the scriptures *over,* and there it will be shown;
The tree that will bear no fruit must be cut down.

Abraham was a man well beloved by the Lord,
He was true to be found in great Jehovah's word,
He stretched forth his hand and took a knife to slay his son,
An angel appearing said The Lord's will be done!

0, Abraham! 0, Abraham! Lay no hand upon the lad,
He sent him onto thee to make my heart glad;
Thy seed shall increase like stars in the sky,
And thy soul into heaven like Gabriel shall fly.

0, *never,* 0, *never* will I hear an orphan cry,
Nor yet a gentle virgin until the day I die;
You wandering Jews that travel the wide world round,
May knock at the door where truth is to be found.

Often against the Turks and infidels, we fight,
To let the wandering world know we're in the right,
For in heaven, there's a lodge, and St. Peter keeps the door,
And none can enter in but those that are pure.

St. Peter opened, and so we entered in,
Into the holy seat secure, which is all free from sin;
St. Peter he opened, and so we entered there,
And the glory of the temple no man can compare.

"VANITY OF VANITIES, ALL IS VANITY" AUTHOR UNKNOWN, FROM A COLLECTION OF CHOICE COUNCILS IN VERSE AND PROSE.

What are life's joys and gains? What pleasures crowd it's ways, That
man should take such pains To seek them all his days?
Sort this unlucky fight.
On which your mind is bent, See if this type of life
Is worth the trouble spent.

Is pride your heart's desire? Is power your climbing aim? Is Love your
folly's fire?
Is wealth your restless game? Pride, power, love, wealth and all, Time's
touchtone shall destroy, And, like a cheap coin, prove all Vain
substitutes for joy.

Do you think that pride exalts,
And hides your faults in other's eyes? Like walking shadow by your side,
Instead becomes your mocking ape.

Do you think that power's disguise Can make you almighty seem?
It may in all fools eyes, But not in worth's esteem:
When all that you can ask,
And all that she can give, Is but all a petty mask.

Go, let the fancies range, And ramble where they may; View power in
every change, And what's the display?
From the lowest shade in power,
To the rulers of the state,
To the meteors of an hour.

View all, and mark the end.
Of every proud extreme,
Where flattery turns a friend,
And counterfeits esteem,
Where worth is copied show,
Like toys of golden glow
That's sold for copper coins.

Ambition's haughty nod,
With fancies may deceive,
They tell you you're a god,
And will you such believe?
Go, bid the seas be dry,
Go, hold Earth like a ball,
Or throw her fancies by,
For God can do it all.

Do you think when wealth is won,
Your heart has its desire?
Hold ice up to the Sun,
And wax before the fire.
Who with riches deals,
And thinks that peace can be bought and sold,
Will find them slippery eels,
That slide is the firmest hold.

Do you think that beauty's power,
Life's sweetest pleasure gives?
Go, pluck the summer flower,
And see how long it lives:
Behold, the rays glide on,
Along the summer plain,
You can't just say they're gone,
And measure beauty's reign.

Look on the brightest eye,
Don't teach it to be proud,
But view the clearest sky
And you shall find a cloud;
Don't call each face you meet
An angel's, just because it's fair,
But look beneath your feet,
And think of what you are.

Who thinks that love does live
In beauty's tempting show,
Shall find his hopes ungive,

And melt in reason's thaw;
Does lawless pleasures grasp?
Judge, not you deal in joy;
It's flower hides the viper,
That reveals to destroy.

Who trusts a harlot's smile,
And by her wiles is led,
Is playing with a sword,
With dung over his head.
Do you doubt my warning song?
Then, doubt the Sun gives light,
Doubt truth to teach you wrong,
And wrong alone as right;
Be a tyrant, or be a slave,
As suits your ends the best.

Or pause amongst the toils,
For visions won and lost,
And count the fancied spoils,
If ever they quit cost;
And if they, still as worthy things, possess your mind,
Pick straws with Bedlam Bess,
And call them diamond rings.

Your folly's past advice,
Your heart's already won,
Your fall's above all price,
So go and be undone;
For all who do prefer the seeming great for small,
Shall make wine into vinegar,
And the sweetest honey vile.

You can profit if you heed these truths I sing,
Clip folly's wanton wing,
And keep her within call;
What you can easily try:
The lesson 'how to live'
Is learning 'how to die.'

"EMERALD TABLETS OF HERMES"
BY: JABIR IBN HAYYAN

Truth Certainty! That in which, there is no doubt! That which is above is
from that which is below, and That which is below is from that which is
above, Working the miracles of one.
As all things were from one.
Its father is in the Sun, and its mother the Moon. The Earth carried it in
her belly,
The Wind nourished it in her belly, As Earth which shall become Fire,
Feed the Earth from that which is subtle and With the greatest power.
It ascends from the Earth to heaven, and It becomes ruler over that
which is above and That which is below.

JABIR IBN HAYYAN (GEBER)

My wealth: let sons and brethren part. Some things they can not share;
My work well done, my noble heart,
These are my own to wear.

PHARAOH AMENEMOPE (EGIPT, REIGN 1001-992 BC)

Incline your ears to my sayings,
And apply your heart to their comprehension.
The truly prudent man, who puts himself aside,
Is like a tree growing in a garden,
He flourishes and multiplies his fruit,
He abides in the presence of his Lord,
His fruit is sweet; his shade is pleasant,
And he will find his end in the garden.
Better is poverty in the hand of God
Than riches in the storehouse.
Weary not yourself to seek for more,
Riches have wings like geese,
And they have flown to heaven.
The skillful scribe in his office,
Shall find himself a worthy high attendant.

EMPEDOCLES (490-430 BC)

Hear first the four roots of all things:
Bright Zeus (fire), life-giving Hera (air),
Aidoneus (earth/Hades) and Nestis (water)
Who moistens the springs of men with her tears.

Second, I will tell you:
There's no origination of anything that is mortal,
Nor any end in death;
Only mixture and separation of what is mixed,
But men call this 'Origination'.

In human form, light is mingled with air,
Or in the form of wild beasts, of plants or of birds,
Men say these things have come into being,
And when they're gone or parted, called evil fate,
So, in accordance with custom, I will call it so.

What was not before can't become,
And what already is can't simply perish.
Love and Strife were before,
So I think, there will not be
Extremely long times without both.

Alone out of many, and other times separated,
So there were many from one;
Fire, Water, Earth, and boundless height of Air;
Apart from these, Strife. As for balance:
Love, among them of equal size to all.

Swift darting Sun and kind Moon
A borrowed light, circular in form,
It revolves around the Earth,
For she beholds opposite to her
The sacred circle of her Lord.

The Moon scatters the Sun's rays into the sky above.
With her gleaming breadth, she spreads darkness over Earth.

Earth comes in front of the lights,
To make the solitary, blind-eyed night.
Many fires burn beneath, and
The sea is the sweat of the Earth.

By earth we see earth, by water we see water,
And air by glorious air so is fire seen by fire, and Love by Love;
Also, strife by strife.
Water (tenacious Love) is increased by water, primaeval fire by fire,
Earth causes its own to increase, and air multiplies air.
To the roots it came from, everything will return;
Our bodies to Earth, our blood to Water, our heat to Fire, and our
breath to the Air.

Tall trees bear fruits, and first are the olives!
Wine is water that fermented in the wood beneath the bark.
Sometimes all is One, rendered loving by Aphrodite,
While other times many, fighting itself by Strife.
Divine Wisdom is the Blessing of life.

We can't draw near God with our eyes,
Or take hold of him with our hands,
For He has no human head or hairy parts,
God is a divine sacred mind, Darting with swift thoughts,
Through the whole world and through it all.

"VENUS AND ADONIS"
BY WILLIAM SHAKESPEARE (1564 - 1616)

Who sees his true Love in her naked bed,
Teaching the sheets a whiter hue than white,
But, when his glutton eye so full has fed,
His other agents aim at like delight?
Who is so faint that dare not be so bold
To touch the fire, the weather being cold?

Let me excuse this warrior and learn of him,
To take advantage of presented joy;
0, learn to Love; the lesson is but plain,
And once made perfect, never lost again.
For misery is trodden on by many,
And being low, never relieved by any.

Love comforts like sunshine after rain,
Love's gentle spring does always fresh remain,
Lust's winter comes eve summer half be done;
Love suffers not; lust like a glutton dies.

Where Love reigns, disturbing jealousy
Does call himself affection's sentinel;
Gives false alarms, suggesting mutiny,
And in a peaceful hour, does cry, "Kill, kill!"
Distempering gentle Love in his desire,
As air and water do abate the fire.

This sour informer, this hate-breeding spy,
This cancer that eats up Love's tender spring,
This carry tale, dissentious jealousy,
That sometime true news, sometimes false does bring,
Knocks at my heart and whispers in my ear
That if I Love you, I your death should fear?

O hard believing Love, how strange it seems
Not to believe, and yet too credulous!
Your weal and woe are both extremes;
Despair and hope make you ridiculous:
The one does flatter you unlikely,
In likely thoughts the other kills you quickly.

Since you are dead, Love, here I prophesy:
Sorrow on Love hereafter shall attend:
It shall be waited on with jealousy,
Find a sweet beginning but the unsavory end,
Never settled equally, but high and low,
That all Love's pleasure shall not match his woe.

It shall be fickle, false and full of fraud,
The bottom poison, and the top over strewn
With sweets that shall the truest sight beguile:
The strongest body shall it make most weak,
Strike the wise dumb and teach the fool to speak.

The string ruffian shall it keep in quiet,
Pluck down the rich, enrich the poor with treasures;
It shall be raging-mad and silly mild,
Make the young old, the old become a child.

It shall suspect where is no cause to fear;
It shall not fear where it should most mistrust;
It shall be merciful and too severe,
And most deceiving when it seems most just;
Perverse, it shall be where it shows most toward,
Put fear to valor, courage to the coward.

It shall be the cause of war and dire events,
And set dissension between the son and father;
Subject and servile to all discontents,
As dry combustions matter is to fire:

Sick in his prime, death does my Love destroy,
They that Love best, their Love they shall not enjoy.

"MERCHANT OF VENICE"
WILLIAM SHAKESPEARE

The man that has no music in himself,
Nor is moved with concord of sweet sounds,
Is fit for treasons, deceit, and spoils:
The motions of his spirit are dull as night.
And his affections dark as Erebus:
Let no such man be trusted.

"TO BE OR NOT TO BE, HAMLET"
BY WILLIAM SHAKESPEARE

To be, or not to be; that is the question:
Whether it's nobler in the mind to suffer
The slings and arrows of outrageous fortune, or
To take arms against a sea of troubles, and
By opposing them, end them?

"CHRISTMAS, HAMLET"
BY WILLIAM SHAKESPEARE

I've heard the cock, trumpet to the morning awake the god of day,
At his warning, whether in sea or fire, in earth or air, the extravagant and
Erring spirit hurries to his confine, and of the truth herein, this present object
 Made probation. It faded on the crowing of the cock; some say that ever
'Against that season comes, wherein our savior's birth is celebrated,
The bird of dawning sings all night long, and then they say no spirit dare stir abroad,
The nights are wholesome, then no planets strike, no fairy takes, nor witch has
Power to charm, so gracious is the time.'

LOVE
BY SHAKESPEARE

Love looks not with eyes but with the mind.
Love is said to be a child, winged cupid painted blind.
Love alters not with brief hours and weeks,
Love is not time's fool,
Love is not Love which alters when it alterations finds,
But bears it out even to the edge of doom.
Such is my love, to you I so belong,
That for your right myself will bear all wrong.

Ladies, down on your knees and thank heaven for a good man's love.
When Love hurts, Love more and more and more until it hurts no more.
Love all, trust few, wrong none.

"HIM TO THE SUN"
FROM THE EGYPTIAN BOOK OF THE DEAD
FROM AROUND 1550 BCE

Homage to you, O Ra (Sun power), at your tremendous rising!
You rise! You shine! The heavens are rolled aside!
you are the King of Gods; you are the All-comprising,
From you we come; in you are deified (glorified)

Your priests go forth at dawn; they wash their hearts with laughter;
Divine winds move in music across your golden strings.
At Sunset, they embrace you as every cloudy rafter (layer)
Flames with reflected colour from your wings.

You sail over the zenith, and your heart rejoices;
Your Morning Boat and Evening Boat with fair winds meet together;
Before your face, the godless Maat (of truth and justice) exalts her fateful
Feather,
And at your name, the halls of Anu (supreme God) ring with voices.

O, you're perfect! You're eternal! You're only One! Great Hawk that flies
with the flying Sun!
Between the Turquoise Sycamores (fig trees) that rises, young forever,
Your image flashing on the bright celestial river.

Your rays are on all faces; You're inscrutable.
Age after age your life renews its eager prime.
Time whirls its dust beneath thee; thou art immutable,
Maker of Time, yourself beyond all Time.

You pass through the portals that close behind the night,
Gladdening the souls of them that lay in sorrow.
The True of Word, the Quiet Heart, arise to drink your light;
You are Today and Yesterday; You are Tomorrow!

Homage to you, O Ra (Sun power) who wakes life from slumber! You rise!
You shine! Your radiant face appears!
Millions of years have passed,-- We can not count their number,--
Millions of years shall come. You are above the years.

"OH WEEP FOR THOSE"
BY LORD BYRON (1788 - 1824)

Oh! weep for those that wept by Babel's stream,
Whose shrines are desolate, whose land a dream,
Weep for the harp of Judah's broken shell_
Mourn_ where their God that dwelt_ The goddess dwell!

And where shall Israel lave (wash) her bleeding feet?
And where shall Zion's songs again seem sweet?
And Judah's melody once more rejoices.
The hearts that leapt before its heavenly voice?

Tribes of the wandering foot and weary brest!
How shall you fly away and be at rest!
The wild_ dove has her nest,_ The fox has his cave_
Mankind, their country_ Israel, but the grave.

"CHILDISH RECOLLECTIONS"
BY LORD BYRON (1788-1824)

"Ah, Sure, some stronger impulse vibrates here
Which whispers friendship will be doubly dear
To one, who thus for kindred hearts must roam,
And seek abroad, the Love denied at home."

"THE SATYRICON" ZODIAC,
BY TITUS PETRONIUS, ITALY (27-66AD)

This heaven in which dwell the twelve gods revolves itself into twelve different configurations and presently becomes the Ram. So whosoever is born under this sign has many flocks and herds and much wool (with profit); a hard head into the bargain, a shameless brow and a sharp horn. Most of you scholars and unscrupulous lawyers are born under this sign. Next, the whole sky becomes Bull; then are born obstinate fellows in charge of the goods and, as such, think of nothing but filling up their own bellies. Under the Twins are born horses in a pair, oxens in a yoke, and men blessed with a sturdy set of testicles, all who manage to keep in with both sides. I was born under the Crab myself. Therefore, I stand on many feet and have many possessions both by sea and by land, for the Crab is equally adapted to either element. And this is why I never put anything on that sign, so as not to eclipse my horoscope. Under the Lion are born great eaters and wasters, and all who love to dominate; under the Virgin, women, runaways and jailbirds; under the Scales, butchers and perfumers and all retail traders; under the Scorpion, poisoners and cutthroats; under the Archer, squint-eyed folks, who look at the greens and whip off the bacon; under Capricorn, hard-working sons for whatever's useful; under Aquarius or the Waterman, are the Innkeepers and Landlords; under Pisces, or the Fishes, fine cooks and fine talkers. Thus the world goes around like a mill, and is forever at some mischief, whether making men or reuniting them.

Ram: Aries	Lion: Leo	The Archer: Sagittarius
Bull: Taurus	Virgin: Virgo	Capricorn [The Sea-goat]
Twins: Gemini	Scales: Libra	The waterman: Aquarius
Crab: Cancer	Scorpion	The Fishes: Pisces

ISAAC WATTS

The Ram, the Bull, the heavenly Twins,
Beneath the Crab, the Lion shines,
The Virgin and the Scales.
The Scorpion, Archer and He-Goat,
The Man that pours the Water out,
And Fish with glittering tails.

"TO BOATSWAIN (EPITAPH TO A DOG)"
BY LORD BYRON (1788-1824)

Near this Spot are deposited the Remains of one who
Possessed Beauty without Vanity,
Strength without Insolence,
Courage without Ferocity,
and all the virtues of Man without his Vices.
This praise, which would be unmeaning Flattery
If inscribed over human Ashes.
Is but a just tribute to the Memory of BOATSWAIN, a DOG.
Who was born in Newfoundland May 1803
 and died at Newstead Nov! 18th. 1808.
When some proud Son of Man returns to Earth.
Unknown to Glory but upheld by Birth,
The sculptor's art exhausts the pomp of woe,
And storied urns record who rests below:
When all is done, upon the Tomb is seen.
But the poor Dog, in life the firmest friend,
The first to welcome, foremost to defend,
Whose laborers fight, live, and breathe for him alone.
Unhonored falls, unnoticed, all his worth.
Denied in heaven the Soul he held on earth:
While man, vain insect! hopes to be forgiven,
And claims himself a sole exclusive heaven,
Oh, man! thou feeble tenant of an hour,
Debased by slavery or corrupt by power.
Who knows thee well must quit thee with disgust,
Degraded mass of animated dust!
 Thy love is lust, thy friendship all a cheat,

Thy tongue hypocrisy, thy heart deceit,
By nature vile, ennobled but by name,
Each kindred brute might bid thee blush for shame.
Ye! who behold perchance this simple urn,
Pass on; it honors none you wish to mourn.
To mark a friend's remains, these stones arise;
I never knew but one - and here he lies.

"HYMN TO APHRODITE 'VENUS"
BY SAPPHO 630/612 BC- 570 BC

Venus, Charming Beauty of the Skies, deathless Aphrodite,
Your throne is cunning craft, ensnarer child of God,
I pray to you, don't subdue with sorrow this poor heart of mine.

Mistress, whenever in the past from far you heard my call
And headed it, stepping out of the paternal home,
Shinning gold, all your radiant charms confessed and rapidly took off.

After harnessing your cart so sweet,
Quick sparrows led you around the dark landscapes,
Feathers densely spinning as a whirlwind,
Heaven's spheres travelling through mid-air all the way down here.

Very soon, they came with you exalted, with an immortal countenance;
your heavenly features smiled and probed me;
What arose that again, did I call for you to make me suffer?

What this frenzied soul desired would happen again
That Love shakes my heart,
Am I being persuaded to give in to love again?
Is Sappho misbehaving?

Now I may still flee, but quickly I shall run to it,
Now, I may refuse all gifts, but soon, if not in Love already,
Willingly or not, I will be in love.

Please come again, but come now to ease my grief
Set me free from all distressing cares;
I beg you, let this soul accomplish all it vowed;
And become yourself my very own ally.

"IF DEATH BE GOOD"
BY SAPPHO

If death be good,
Why do the Gods not die? If life be ill,
Why do the Gods still live? If Love be naught,
Why do the Gods still Love?
If Love be all,
What should men do but Love?

SAPHO WRITES TO PHAON

Two birds, unlike oftentimes
Joined are white doves;
Also, the bird that's green,
black turtle loves.

"MITHRAIC CEREMONIES"
AUTHOR UNKNOWN

A broad-leaved olive decks the haven's head,
Near a cave; how lovely! But how dark!
The holy place of Nymphs, the Naids called.
There goblets are, and jars of marble made.
Wherein the honeybee constructs its cells:
There, too, long looms of stone,
On which the Nymphs sea-purple garments weave,
A wond'rous sight.
Fountains it has eternal, and
Two gates,
The northern one to men Admittance gives,
That to the South is more divine_
A way untrod by men_
To immortals only known.

"THE GATES"
BY UNKNOWN

Two gates at Cancer and Capricorn,
By Plato are called 'The Two Doors'.
Of these Cancer is the one by which souls come down, and
Capricorn that by which they again go up.
They are in the South and the North and
The most humid ones in the South.

Cancer being in the North and the sign of
Summer Solstice, and is the way by which souls descend, and
The way to the abode of the Gods is by Capricorn, which is
The South and the sign of Winter Solstice
"The Gates", which look towards the North, are rightly said to be
Open to the descent of men, but the southern quarter is not merely
The way of the Gods. For which Homer does not say:
The way of the Gods but of 'Immortals'.

EMPEROR MARCUS AURELIUS WRITINGS (121 AD-180AD)

Everything harmonizes with me,
which is harmonious to you.
Nothing for me is too early or too late,
Which is in due time for you.
Everything is fruit to me,
 Which the seasons bring.
O, Nature: from you are all things,
To you, all things return.

Apply to: Just thoughts, social acts,
Words that never lie
And a disposition that
Gladly accepts all that happens,
As necessary, as usual,
As flowing from a principle and
Source of the same kind.

On every occasion that leads to vexation,
Remember that it is not a misfortune, but
That to bear it nobly is good fortune.

Within all things held together by Nature,
There is within the power which made them,
Which It's fit to reverence.

All things are connected, and the bond is Holy.
There's one Universe made up of all things,
One God, One substance, One law,
One common reason in all,
One truth, One perfection for all.

Be simple, be modest and kind,
Indifferent to all that comes between Virtue and Vice.
Love mankind, follow God, that law rules all;
And remember that: "Law rules ALL."

"DESTINY" FROM THE SOPHOCLES PLAY BY: MENELAUS, GREEK RULER, HUSBAND TO HELEN OF TROY

For me, Destiny, alas,
Is found whirling upon God's swift wheel around, and
Changing still and as the Moon's fair frame
Can't continue for two nights the same.
But out of shadow first, a crescent shows, and
Thence into beauty and perfection grows, and
When the form of plenitude it wears,
Dwindles again, and wholly disappears.

"ARCHILOCHUS VERSES" BY ARCHILOCHUS (GREECE 680-645 BC)

I am the servant of Lord Enyalius (Ares, God of War)
Skilled in the lovely gift of Muses.

My soul, my soul,
All disturbed by sorrows, inconsolable;
Bear up, hold out,
Meet front on the many foes that brush on you;
Now, from this side and now that side,
Enduring all such strife up close;
Never wavering, and
Should you win, don't openly exult,
Nor, defeated, throw yourself lamenting in a heap at home.
 Delight in things that are delightful, and
In hard times, grieve not too much_
Appreciate the rhythm that controls men's lives.

Mars and the muses friends alike designed:
To arts and arms, indifferently inclined.

The fox knows many things,
The hedgehog only the one 'big' thing.

"FROM EPICTETUS WRITINGS" GREEK (55-135AD) BORN INTO SLAVERY TO BECOME SAGE.

We are not forever; we are not eternity.
We are human beings,
Members of the whole and as the hour is part of the day,
We must come like the hour and like the hour must pass.
'Lead me, O God, and you, O Destiny,
Be what it may be, the goal appointed me. I will follow, bravely or not.

What you Love is not your own; it is given for the present, not forever.
You were not born when you chose. You were born when the world had need of you.
The life entangled with Fortune is like a torrent,
Turbulent and muddy, hard to pass, masterful of mood, Noisy and of brief continuance.
In life or death: To a good man, there is no evil.
Without God, put your hands into nothing.

ST. FRANCIS OF ASSISI (1181-1226)

Praise you, my Lord, for all Thy creatures,
Above all, Brother Sun
Who brings us the day and lends us his light.
His radiant splendor speaks to us of Thee, O most high.

Lord, make me an instrument of your peace,
Where there is hatred, let me sow love;
Where there is injury, pardon;
Where there is doubt, faith;
Where there is despair, hope;
Where there is darkness, light;
And where there is sadness, joy.

O Divine Master, Grant that I may
Not so much seek to be consoled as to console;
To be understood as to understand;
To be loved as to love.
For it is in giving that we receive;
It is in pardoning that we are pardoned;
And it is in dying that we are born.

JUDAS THOMAS (JESUS CHRIST'S FIRST DISCIPLE)

It is to those who are worthy of my mysteries that I tell my mysteries.

Do not let your left hand know what your right hand is doing.

If two make peace with each other in this one house,
They will say to the mountain: 'Move away', and it will move away.

Whoever blasphemes against the Father will be forgiven, and
Whoever blasphemes against the Son will be forgiven, but
Whoever blasphemes against the Holy Spirit,
Will 'not' be forgiven either on Earth or in Heaven?

To look for the end, you must look where the beginning is,
For where the beginning is, there will be the end.
Blessed is who will take his place in the beginning,
He will know the end and will not experience death.

Recognize what is in your plain sight, and that,

Which is hidden from you will become plain,
For there is nothing hidden which will not become manifest.

Blessed are the solitary and elect, for you will find the kingdom.
For you are from it, and to it you will return.

The images are manifest to man, but the light in them
Remains concealed in the image of the light of the Father.
He will become manifest, but His image will remained
Concealed by His Light.

Heaven will not come by waiting for it. Rather, the Kingdom of the Father is
Spread out upon the Earth, and men don't see it.

"Become passersby"

THE BIBLE - ROMANS 1 CORINTHIANS

God has chosen the foolish things of the world to confound the wise, And
God has chosen the weak things of the world to confound
The things that are mighty.

ANGELUS SILESIUS (JOHANN SCHEFFLER)

Everyone to his own. The bird is in the sky,
The stone rests on the land; in water lives the fish,
My spirit in God's hand.

THE OLD MAN'S WISH (WALTER POPE 1630-1714)

May I govern my passions with absolute sway,
And grow wiser and better as strength wears away,
Without gout or stone, by a gentle decay.

VERSES TO FRIENDS- JOHN POMFRET (1667-1702)

Adore the hand that gives the blow.

BENEDICT (BARUCH) SPINOZA (1632-1704)

One and the same thing can, at the same time

Be good, bad and indifferent,
Music is good for melancholy,
Bad for mourning,
And not good or bad for the deaf.

"THE MIND OF THE FRONT' FROM 'THE HISTORY OF THE WORLD
WALTER RALEIGH (1552 OR 1554-1618) AND "UNDERWOODS" BEN JOHNSON

From death and dark oblivion
The mistress of man's life,
Grave HISTORY, raising the
World to good or evil FAME
Does vindicate it to ETERNITY.

7High PROVIDENCE would do:
That nor the good might be
Defrauded, nor the great secured, but
Does might know their ways are
Understood, and the reward, and
Punishment assured.

This makes that lighted by the
Beamy hand of TRUTH, which
Searches the most hidden springs
And guided by EXPERIENCE,
Whose straight wand, does mete (dispense),
Whose LINE does found the
Depth of things.

She cheerfully supports what
She rears: Assisted by no strengths,
But are her own. Some note of
Which, as proper titles, she is known.
Times witness, herald of
Antiquity, the light of TRUTH,
And life of MEMORY.

"THE NYMPH'S REPLY TO THE PASSIONATE SHEPHERD"
SIR WALTER RALEIGH

If all the world and love were young and truth in every shepherd's tongue,
These pretty pleasures might make me move, to live with you and be your
love.

"THE LIE" BY
SIR WALTER RALEIG

Go, Soul, the body's guest,
Upon a thankless errand,
Fear not to touch the best;
The truth shall be your warranty;
Go, since I must die;
And give the world the lie.

Tell the high power it glows
And shines like rotten wood;
Tell the church it shows
What's good and does no good:
If high power and church reply,
Then, give them both the lie.

Tell the government they live and
Act by others' action;
Not loved unless they give,
Not strong, but by a group.
If the government replies,
Then give them all the lie.

Tell the men in power,
That manage corporations,
Their purpose is ambition,
Their practice only hates:
And if they once reply,
Then give them all the lie.

Tell those that brave it most,
They beg for more by spending,
Who, at their greatest cost,

Seek nothing but commending.
And if they do reply,
Then give them all the lie.

Tell zeal it wants devotion;
Tell Love it is but lust;
Tell time it measures only motion;
Tell flesh it is but dust (And wish they don't reply)
For you must give the lie.

Tell age it daily wastes;
Tell honor how it alters;
Tell beauty how she flies;
Tell favor how it falters:
And as they shall reply:
Give everyone the lie.

Tell wit how much it argues
In tickle points of niceness,
Tell wisdom she entangles
Herself in over wiseness:
And when they do reply:
Straight give them both the lie.

Tell medicine of her boldness;
Tell skill it is pretension;
Tell charity of coldness;
Tell law it's controversy:
And as they do reply:
So give them still the lie.

Tell Fortune of her blindness;
Tell Nature of decay;
Tell Friendship of unkindness;
Tell Justice of delay:

And if they reply:
Then give them all the lie.

Tell Art it has no soundness,
But varies by esteem;
Tell schools they lack profoundness,
And stand too much on seeming:
If Art and schools reply,
Give Art and schools the lie.

Tell Faith that it has fled the city;
Tell The Country how it errs and strays;
Tell Manhood that he shakes off pity
And tell Virtue that she least prefers:
And if they do reply,
Spare not to give the lie.

So when you have done,
The blabber I've commanded
Although to give the lie
Deserves no less than stabbing--
Stab at your free will,
Because no stab can kill the soul.

"MUSICAL HARMONY"
CORNELIUS AGR IPPA (1486-1535)

Musical Harmony is a powerful conceiver. It can celestial influences allure.
It can change affections, intentions, notions, actions, and dispositions.
Lake Alexandria's fish delight with its harmonious sounds; It has caused
friendship between men and dolphins, Playing the harp affects the
Hyperborean swans. Melodious voices tame the Indian elephants.
The elements themselves delight with sweet, harmonious sound.

"THE FOREST'
BY BEN JOHNSON, UNITED KINGDOM (1572-1637)

Not to know vice at all is virtue and not fate;
Next to that virtue is to know vice well, And
Her black spite spell (and since no breast is safe)
We must plant a guard of thoughts to watch
At the ports of mind: The eye and ear.
That no strange, unkind object arrives.
But the heart, our spy, gives instant knowledge
To wakeful reason, who will quickly taste the treason,

And commit desire, armed with bow, shaft and fire;

Inconstant like the sea where it's born And like a
A rough, swelling storm rides on the surge of fear and boils.
Now, in true Love, no such effects will show.
Love is far more gentle, fine, pure, perfect, no divive!
It's a golden chain let down from heaven,
Whose links are bright and even,
That falls like sleep on lovers and combines:
The soft, sweet minds in equal knots: This bears no brands,
Nor darts to murder different hearts, but in calm and
God, like unity, preserves community.
0, who is he that in this peace enjoys the elixir of all joys?
Who, blessed with such a high chance, would, at the suggestion of
Desire cast himself from all this happiness?
But, I hear some vicious fool draw near,
That cries and swears: There's no such thing!
Who can so abstain? Makes blessed gain.
He that for Love of goodness hates ill,
Is more crown-worthy still,
Than he, which for his sin's penalty forbears;
His heart sins, though he fears.
But, a person like our Dove, graced with Phoenix' Love;
A beauty of that clear and sparkling light Would make a day of night, and
turn the blackest sorrows, to bright joys; and whose breath destroys all
taste of bitterness.

"THE DEER'S CRY (THE BREASTPLATE OF ST. PATRICK"

St. PATRICK: ROMANO- CHRISTIAN MISSIONARY (387-460 AD) LEGEND:

**ST. PATRICK SANG THIS HYMN WHEN KING LEARY'S MEN CAME TO KILL HIM, BUT ALL THE ASSAILANTS SAW WAS WILD DEER AND A FAWN. APPARENTLY BECAUSE OF THIS PRAYER:

I arise today through a mighty strength, the invocation of the Trinity, through belief in the Threeness, through confession of the Oneness of the Creator of creation.

I arise today through the strength of Christ with his Baptism, through the strength of His Crucifixion with His burial, through the strength of his Resurrection with His Ascension, through the strength of His descent for the Judgment of Doom.

I arise today through the strength of the Love of Cherubim, in obedience of Angels, in the service of Archangels, in hope of resurrection to meet with reward, in prayers of Patriarchs, in predictions of Prophets, in preachings of Apostles, in faith of Confessors, In innocence of Holy Virgins, in deeds of righteous men.

I arise today through the strength of Heaven: Light of Sun, brilliance of Moon, splendor Of Fire, speed of Lightning, swiftness of Wind, depth of Sea, stability of Earth, firmness of Rock.

I arise today through God's strength to pilot me: God's might uphold me, God's Wisdom to guide me, God's eye to look before me, God's ear to hear me, God's word to Speak for me, God's hand to guard me, God's way to lie before me, God's shield to Protect me, God's host to secure me: 'Against snares of devils, against temptations of vices, against inclinations of nature, against everyone who shall wish me ill, afar and near, alone and in a crowd'.

I summon today all these powers between me (and these evils): 'Against every cruel and merciless power that may oppose my body and my Soul, Against incantations of false prophets, against black laws of heathenry, against false laws of heretics, against craft and idolatry, against spells of women (any witch) and Smiths and wizards, against every knowledge that endangers man's body and Soul. Christ to protect me today against poison, against burning, against drowning, against Wounding, so that there may come abundance of reward.

Christ with me, Christ before me, Christ behind me, Christ in me, Christ beneath me, Christ above me, Christ on my right, Christ on my left, Christ in breadth, Christ in length, Christ in the mouth of every man who speaks of me, Christ in every eye that sees me, Christ in every ear that hears me.

I arise today through a mighty strength, the invocation of the Trinity, through belief in the Threeness, through confession of the Oneness of the Creator of Creation.
Salvation is of the Lord. Salvation is of the Lord.
Salvation is of Christ. May Thy Salvation, 0 Lord, be ever with us.

"FROM PARADISE LOST"

BY JOHN MILTON, ENGLAND (1608-1674)

Of Man's first disobedience, and the fruit
Of that forbidden tree whose mortal taste
Brought taste into the world, and all our woe,
With loss of Eden, till one greater
Man Restore us, and regain the blissful Seat,
Sing Heavenly Muse..

I sung of Chaos and Eternal Night,
Taught by the heavenly Muse to venture down,
The dark descent, and up to reascend..

Should God create another Eve, and I
Another Rib afford, yet loss of thee
Would never from my heart; no, no, I feel

The Link of Nature draws me: Flesh of Flesh,
Bone of my Bone you are, and from your state
Mine never shall be parted, bliss or woe.

All who have their reward on Earth, the fruits of painful
Superstition and blind zeal, only seeking but the praise of
Men, here find fit retribution, empty as their deed.

Is it true, O Christ in heaven, that the highest suffer most?
That the strongest, wander furthest and most hopelessly are lost? That the
mark for rank in Nature is capacity for Pain?
And that the anguish of the singer makes the sweetest line?
'Yet he who reigns within himself, and rules his
Passions, desires, and his fears; is like King'

"HOW MY LIGHT IS SPENT"
JOHN MILTON

When I consider how my light is spent,
Here half my days in this dark world and wide,
And that one talent which is death to hide,
Lodged with me useless, though my soul more bent,
To serve my maker and present my true account, in case He reproves 'Does
God demand day-labor light denied?
That murmur soon replies: God doesn't need either man's work or His own
gifts. Who best bears his mild yoke serve him best
They also serve who just stand and wait.

"THE RUBAIYAT"
BY OMAR KHAYYAM, PERSIA (1048-1131)

Alas, for that cold heart, that never with Love glows,
Nor ever that charming madness knows;
No days are wasted half as much as those!

Ten Powers, and nine spheres, eight heavens made He,
Planets seven, of six sides, as we see,
Five senses, and four elements, three souls,
Two worlds, but only one, 0 man like thee.

Kindness to friends and enemies is well to show,
No kind heart can prove unkind.

Harshness will alienate a close friend,
And Kindness can a deadly enemy reconcile.

To lovers true, what matters dark or fair?
Or if the loved one silk or rags should wear,
 Or lie on down on dust, or rise to heaven?
Yes, would she sink to hell, he'll seek her there.

Allah has promised wine in Paradise,
 Why then should wine on Earth be deemed a vice?
 An Arab in his cups cut Hamzah's girths..

For that sole cause, was drink declared a sin.

If the heart knew life's secrets here below,
At death would know God's secrets too;
But, if you know nothing here, while still yourself,
Tomorrow, stripped of self, what can you know?

The Ball no question makes of Ayes and Noes,
But Here or There as strikes the Player goes;
And He that tossed you down into the Field,
He knows about it all_He knows_He knows!

From mosque outcast, and to church a foe,
Allah, from what clay did you mold me so?
Love's devotee, not Muslims here you see
No silk, but faces wan and rags have we.

Hearts with the light of Love illumined well,
Whether in a mosque or synagogue, they dwell,
Have their names written in the book of Love,
Unvexed by hopes of heaven of fears of hell.

Fortune's smiles are full of tricks, beware!
Her blade is sharp, take care!
If she ever drops a treat into your mouth,
It's poisonous to swallow it, abstain!

Be very wary in the Soul's domain,
And on the world's affairs your lips refrain;
Be, as if you were without eyes, tongue and ears.
While eyes, tongue and ears you still retain.

Crave no worldly sweets to take you fill, or
Wait a turn on fortune, good or ill,
Be of light heart, as are the skies above,
They roll a round or two, and then lie still.

Heed not the Sunnah, or the law divine;
If to the poor his portion you assign,
And never injure one, nor yet abuse,
I guarantee you heaven, and now some wine!

To wise and worthy men your life devote,
But from the worthless keep your walk remote;
Dare to take poison from a sage's hand,
But from a fool refuse an antidote.

Don't let greed enslave the mind,
Or vain ambition bind you,
Be sharp as fire, as running water swift,
Not, like the earth's dust, the sport of every wind!

Of Wisdom's dictates, two are best,
Surpassing all traditions and trends;
Better to fast than eat of every meat,
Better to live alone than mate with all!
Don't hold your grief and despair,
But in this unjust world, be just and fair;
Know all things you set your heart upon
Sooner or later, must the Soul destroy!

Love, could you and I, with Him, conspire
To grasp this sorry Scheme of Things entire,
Would not we shatter it to bits and then
Remold it nearer to the Heart's Desire!

My true condition I may this way explain,
In two short verses which the whole contain
'From Love to You know lay down my life,
In hope your Love will raise me up again.'

"Oh Thou who burns in the Heart for those who burn
In Hell, whose fires thyself shall feed in turn.
How long be crying, 'Mercy on them, God!
Why, who art Thou to teach, and He to learn?''

"If I myself upon a looser Creed
Have loosely strung the Jewel of Good deed,
Let this one thing for my Atonement plead:

That One for Two I never did misread."

"ILLUSION SYMB"
BY OMAR KHAYYAM

For in and out, above, below,
This is nothing but a magic shadow show,
Played in a box whose candle is the Sun,
Round and round which, we phantom figures come and go.

BOETHIUS

Each thing a certain course and laws obeys,
Striving to turn back to his proper place;
Nor any settled order can be found,
But that which doth within itself embrace
The births and ends of all things in a round.

KEATS

Heard melodies are sweet, but those unheard are sweeter,
Therefore, yet sweet pipes, play on...
When old age shall this generation waste,
You shall remain, in between of other worries than ours,
A friend to man, to whom you say:
'Beauty is truth. Truth beauty.'
That is all you know on Earth and all you need to know.

VIRGIL, ITALY (70-19 BC)

Look with favor upon bold beginnings;
And you, sister 'Muse',
Whom I Love with the sacred fervor all worlds above,
0 take me to your seer:
Give me the ways of wandering stars to know
The depths of heaven above and earth below.
Let me know the paths Sidereals and the Moon's New birth,
The Sun's eclipses, and the pangs of Earth.
To know the force that rises tides overflows the marsh,

And makes the waves subside;

Why the Sun in winter hurries to his rest, and by
What laws are summer nights compressed.
I know Heaven, Earth, the Moon's pale orb, and
The starry train are nourished by a Soul,
A bright intelligence whose flame glows
In each member of the frame,
And stirs the mighty whole.
That earthward they may pass once more,
Remembering not the things before,
And with a blind propension,
Yearn to fleshly bodies to return.
The signs of the old flame, I know them well.

I pray that the Earth's gape is deep enough,
To take me down, or that the Almighty Father
Blast me with one bolt to the shades, the pit of night,
Before I dishonor you, my Conscience, and break your laws.

Fortunate minds have the power to probe
Causes of things and trample underfoot,
All terrors of inexorable Fate.
Time is flying, never to return.
Love conquers all, Love begets Love,
Love knows no rules; this is the same for all;
Therefore, let us submit to Love.
Your descendants will gather your fruits.

"PARADISO, PURGATORIO"
BY DANTE

O, grace abounding and allowing me to dare,
To fix my gaze on Eternal Light
So deep my vision was consumed in it

I saw how it contains within it's depth
All things bound in a single book by Love
Of which creation is the scattered leaves:

How substance, accident and their relation
Were fused in such a way that what I now
Describe is but a glimmer of that Light.

Madness it is to hope that human minds
Can ever understand the infinity
That comprehends Three Persons in One Being.

Soon you will be where your own eyes will see
The source and cause give you
Their own answer to the mystery.

Be satisfied with this unexplained,
O human race! If you knew everything,
No need for Mary to have born a son.

"PHOENIX" BY OVID

All birds from others do derive their birth,
But yet one foule there is in all of the Earth,
Called by the Assyrians Phoenix,
Who the wain of age repairs,
And sows herself again.

"SEVERAL QUESTIONS ANSWERED"
BY: WILLIAM BLAKE, ENGLAND (1757-1827)

What is it men in women require?
The lineaments and features of gratified desire.
What is it women do in men do require?
The lineaments and features of gratified desire.

The look of Love alarms,
Because it's filled with fire;
But the look of soft deceit
Shall win the lover's hire.

Soft deceit and idleness
These are Beauty's sweetest dresses.

He who binds to himself a joy
Does the winged life destroy;
But he who kisses the joy as it flies,
Lives in Eternity's sunrise.

TO THE MUSES
BY WILLIAM BLAKE

Whether on Ida's shady brow
Or in the chambers of the East
The chambers of the Sun that now
From ancient melody have ceased;

Whether in heaven you wander fair
Or the green corners of the Earth
Or the blue regions of the air
Where the melodious winds have birth;

Whether on crystal rocks, you rove
Beneath the bosom of the sea
Wandering in many a coral grove;
Fair Nine forsaking Poetry;

How have you left the ancient Love
That tribal poet enjoyed in you!
The languid strings scarcely move
The sound is forced the lines are few.

"YOU DON'T BELIEVE"
BY WILLIAM BLAKE

You don't believe, and I won't attempt to make you
You are asleep, and I won't attempt to wake you.
Dream on, dream on while in your pleasant dreams
Of Reason, you may drink of Life's clear streams.
Reason and Newton, they are quite two things;
For so, the sparrow and the swallow sing.

Reason says 'Miracle' Newton says 'Doubt'
Aye! that's the way to make all Nature out.
Doubt, doubt, and don't believe without experiment.
That is the very thing Jesus meant when he said:
"Only believe, believe and try!
Try, try and never mind why!"

"AUGURIES (DIVINATIONS) OF INNOCENCE"
BY WILLIAM BLAKE

To see a world in a grain of sand and a heaven in a wild flower,
Hold infinity in the palm of your hand and eternity in an hour.
A robin redbreast in a cage puts all heaven in a rage.
A dove-house filled with doves and pigeons shudders hell through all its regions.
A dog starved at his master's gate predicts the ruin of the state.
A horse misused upon the road calls to heaven for human blood.
Each outcry of the hunted hare, A fiber from the brain tears.
A skylark wounded in the wing, a cherubim does cease to sing.
The game cock clipped and armed for a fight does the rising Sun frights.
Every wolf's and lion's howl raises from hell a human soul.
The wild deer wandering here and there, keeps the human soul from care.
The lamb misused breeds public strife and yet forgives the butcher's knife.
The bat that flits at the close of eve has left a brain that won't believe it.
The owl that calls upon the night speaks the unbeliever's fright.
He who the ox to wrath has moved shall never be by a woman loved.
The wanton boy who kills the fly shall feel the spider's enmity.
He who torments the chafer's sprite weaves a bower in endless night.
The caterpillar on the leaf, repeats to you your mother's grief.

Kill not the moth nor butterfly, for the Last Judgment draws nearby.
He who shall train the horse to war shall never pass the polar bar.
The beggar's dog and widow's cat, feed them and you will grow fat.
The gnat that sings his summer's song, Poison, gets from Slander's tongue.
The poison of the snake and newt Is the sweat of Envy's foot.
The poison of the honey bee is the artist's jealousy.

The prince's robes and beggar's rags are toadstools on scrooge's bags.
A truth that's told with bad intent beats all the lies you can invent.
It is right it should be so: Man was made for joy and sorrow;
And when this we rightly know, through the world we safely go.
Joy and grief are woven fine, a clothing for the soul divine.
Under every grief and longing runs a silk-stringed joy.
Every tear from every eye becomes a babe for all eternity.
The babe that weeps the rod beneath writes revenge! In realms of death.
The beggar's rags fluttering in the air does to rags the heaven tear.
The soldier, armed with a sword and gun, strikes the summer's Sun.
The poor man's penny is worth more than all the gold on Africa's shore.
Senseless effort squeezed out of laborer's hands,
Shall buy and sell a scrooges land; or
If protected from on high, does that whole nation sell and buy?
He who mocks the infant's faith shall be mocked in age and death.
The child's toys and the old man's reasons are the fruit of the two seasons.
The questioner who sits so sly shall never know how to reply.
He who replies to words of doubt does put the light of knowledge out. The
strongest poison ever known came from Caesar's laurel crown.
Nothing can deform the human race, like when a man is forced to iron
chains.
A riddle, or the cricket's cry, is to doubt a fit reply.
The ant's inch and eagle's mile make lame philosophy to smile.
He who doubts from what he sees, will never believe, do what you please.
If the Sun and Moon could doubt, they'd immediately go out.
To be in a passion you good may do, but not if a passion is in you.
The whore and gambler, by the state-licensed, build that nation's fate.
Every night and every morn, some misery are born.
Every morn and every night, some are born to sweet delight and
Some are born to endless nights.
We are let to believe a lie when we see not through the eye;
Which was born in a night, to perish in a night, when the soul slept in
beams of light.
God appears, and God is light to those poor souls who dwell in the night.
But does a human form display to those who dwell in realms of day?

ANCIENT MAGIC,
AESCHYLUS P.V.

He who learns must suffer. Even
In our sleep, the pain that can't forget
Falls drop by drop upon the heart,
And in our own despair, against our will,
Comes Wisdom to us by
The tough grace of God.

Oh, the torment bred in the race,
The grinding scream of death
And the stroke that hits the vein,
The hemorrhage none can stop, the grief
The curse no man can bear.

Poor men, their destiny. When all goes well, a shadow will overthrow it
If it is unkind, one stroke of a wet sponge wipes the picture out;
And that is by far the most unhappy thing of all.
To tame the savageness of man is to make gentle the life of this world.

At home, there tarries like a lurking snake,
Biding its time, a wrath unreconciled,
A wily watcher, passionate to quench in blood,
The resentment for a murdered child.

But there is a cure in the house, and not outside it, no,
Not from others but from them,
Their bloody strife; We sing to you,
Dark gods beneath the earth.

Now, hear your blissful powers underground.
Answer the call and send help.
Bless the children; give them triumph now.

But Fortune governed all their works,
Till when I first found out how stars did set and rise,
A profitable Art to mortal men;
And others of like use I did devise,
As letters to compose learned wise.
I did teach and first did amplify
The mother of the Muses, Memory.
Memory: mother of all wisdom.

LUCIUS ANNAEUS SENECA (4BC-65AD)

Gold tests with fire,
Woman with gold,
Man with a woman.
Fidelity bought with money,
Money can destroy.

Life speeds on with hurried steps,
And with winged days, the wheel of
The headlong year is turned.

As we wait to live...Life passes on
What we really live is quite small,
The rest is not life, only time.

Who values time?
Who values each day?
Who understands daily death?
Death passes on, and all the years behind us,
Are in death's hands.

Life will follow the path it started upon.
Life will neither reverse nor check it's own course;
It doesn't make noise or remind me how fast it goes;
It silently glides on.

Time won't prolong on command,
Or applaud on popular demand.
Just as on the first day it started, so it will run;
With no delaying or turn.

AVICENA (980-1037)

Up from Earth's center through the seventh gate,
I rose and on the throne of Saturn state,
And many knots unraveled by the road,
But not: 'The master knot of human fate.'

GEORGE WASHINGTON

Labor to keep alive in your breast, that
Little spark of Celestial Fire,
Called Conscience.

Anything will give up it's secrets if you Love it enough,
Not only have I found that when I talk to the little flower
Or to the little peanut, they will give up their secrets, but
I have found that when I silently commune with people
They give up their secrets, too, If you Love them enough.

MAGICAL PHILOSOPHICAL PRECEPTS
Psel.4.
FROM THE CHALDAEAN ORACLES OF ZOROASTER

Direct not your mind to the vast measures of the Earth;
For the plant of truth is not upon the ground.
Nor measure the measures of the Sun, collecting rules,
For he is carried by the eternal will of the Father, not for your sake.
Dismiss the impetuous course of the moon, for she
Runs always by the works of necessity.
The progression of the stars was not generated for your sake.
The wide aerial flight of birds is not true,
Nor the dissection of the entrails of victims: they are all mere toys.
The basis of mercenary fraud: flee from these;
If you would, open the sacred paradise of piety
Where virtue, wisdom and equity assemble.

THUS SPOKE ZARATHUSTRA

To lone dwellers, I sing my song,
Those who can hear the unheard.
Since more dangers are to be found in men than in animals,
Let my animals lead,
The Eagle, the proudest animal under the Sun,
And the Snake, the wisest.
I then ask my pride to go always with my wisdom!
And if my wisdom should someday forsake me:
0 how it loves to fly away,
May my pride then fly away with my folly!

Careless, mocking, and forceful, so does
Wisdom wish us, for she is a woman,
And 'never' Loves anyone but a Warrior.

Man is a rope
Stretched between beast and angel,
A rope over an abyss.
A dangerous crossing,
Dangerous trembling and halting,
Dangerous looking back,
Man is the bridge, not the goal.

Work, for work, is a pastime,
But be careful that pastime should hurt one.
Don't become rich or poor,
To rule or obey, they are both burdensome.

"COSMOS"
D.H. LAURENCE

The Cosmos is a vast Jiving body of which we're still parts.
The Sun is a great heart whose tremors run through our smallest veins.
The Moon is a Great Nerve Center from which we quiver forever.
Who knows the power that Saturn has over us or Venus?
But it's a vital power, rippling exquisitely through us all the time.

HAFEZ DIVAN, PERSIA, (1325-1389 CE)

If, at last, you attain the desire of your life,
Cast the world aside, yea, abandon it!

To them that here renowned by virtue live,
A heavenly palace is the meet reward;
To me, give the Temple of The Grape with red wine stored!

Look upon all the market's gold,
Look at the tears the world has shed in vain,
Will they not satisfy your craving heart?

I have enough of loss, enough of gain;
I have my Love; what more can I obtain?

Night is with child! Haven't you heard?
Night is with child! What will she bring to birth?
I will sit and ask the stars.

Love at last exists, yet if Love were not,
Heart and Soul would sink to the common lot
All things are nought.

The span of your life is as five little days,
Rest softly, ah rest! While the shadow delays.
The powers of the world endure for an hour;
Learn this: Proudest heads shall bend, and dwellers
On the threshold of a friend, be crowned with the dust that crowns the
meek.

The Sultan's crown, with priceless jewels set,
Encircles fear of death and constant dread.
It's best to hide your face from those who long for yours.

Ah, seek the treasure of a mind at rest,
And store it in Ease's treasure chest.

Ask not one grain of favor;
Two hundred sacks of jewels are not worth Your Soul's disgrace.

Parting goes before all meetings,
And then from darkness comes the light.

ATTAR NISHAPUR, PERSIA (1145-1221)

I shall grasp the soul's skirt by the hand and stamp
On the world's head with my foot.
I shall trample Matter and Space with my horse,
Beyond all being, I shall utter a shout,
And then, I should be alone with him.

ATTAR

If while looking in your heart,
You for Self-whole, mistake your shadow part,
That shadow part indeed into the Sun
Shall melt, but senseless of its Union;
But in that Mirror, if with pure eyes
Your Shadow, you for Shadow recognize,
Then shall you back into your center fall
A conscious Ray of that eternal All.

ATTAR

The whole world is a marketplace for Love,
Nothing that is from Love remains remote.
Eternal wisdom made all things in Love:
On Love they all depend, to Love all turn.
The Earth, the heavens, the Sun, the Moon, the stars
The center of their orbit find in Love.
By Love are all bewildered, stupefied,
Intoxicated by the Wine of Love.
From each a mystic silence Love demands,
What do all seek so earnestly? It's Love.
Love is the subject of their inmost thoughts,
In Love, no longer 'You' and 'I' exist.
For self has passed away in the Beloved.
Now, I will draw aside the veil from Love,
And in the temple of my inmost Soul
Behold the Friend, Incomparable Love.
He who would know the secret of both worlds

Will find the secret of them both, is Love.

ATTAR

The Sum of my Perfection is a Glass
Wherein from Seeing into Being pass
All who, reflecting as reflected see
Themselves in Me, and Me in Them: not Me,
But all of Me that a contracted Eye
Is comprehensive of Infinity:
Not yet Themselves: no Selves, but of The All
Fractions, from which they split and whither fall.
*As Water, lifted from the Deep, again
*Falls back in individual Drops of Rain
*Then melts into the Universal Main.
All you have been, and seen, and done, and thought,
Not You but I, have seen and been wrought,
I was the Sin that from Myself rebelled:
I the Remorse that toward Myself compelled:
 I was Tajidar who led the Track:
I was the little Briar that pulled you back:
Sin and Contriction_Retribution owed,
And canceled_Pilgrim, Pilgrimage, and Road,
Was but Myself toward Myself: and Your

Arrival but Myself at my own Door:
Who in your Fraction of Myself behold
Myself within the Mirror Myself hold
To see Myself in, and each part of Me
That sees himself, though drowned, shall ever see.
Come you lost Atoms to your Center draw,
And be the Eternal Mirror that you saw:
Rays that have wandered into Darkness wide
Return, and back into your Sun subside.

THE TETRACTYS IN PYTHAGOREAN PRAYER

Bless us divine number, you, who generated gods and men. Holy, holy
Tetractys, You that contain the root and source of eternally flowing
creation! For the divine
The number begins with profound, pure unity until it comes to the holy
hour. Then it
Begets the mother of all, the all comprising, all bounding, firstborn; never
Swerving, never tiring holy ten, key holder of all.

EMPEROR HADRIAN'S POEM

Roving amiable little soul,
Body's companion and guest;
Now descending for parts,
Colorless, unbending and bare
Your usual distractions are no more shall be there.

"METANOIA"

BY LAOZI, TAO TE CHING (6TH CENTURY BC)

Be humble, and you will remain whole.
Be bent, and you will remain straight.
Be vacant, and you will remain full.
Be worn, and you will remain new.
He who has little will receive.
He who has much will be ashamed.
Therefore, the sage keeps to One,
To become the standard for the world.

ELIAS ASHMOLE

In Astrology, there are (I confess) shallow Brooks through
Which young tyros may wade, but withal there are deep Fords,
Over which the Giants themselves must swim.

SIMON FORMAN

If you will be a good physician
And judge a sickness, right
Mark, well, what I do write to you,
For urine is of little might, But study well Astronomy,
The course of heavens all right to know
For they will tell you certainly
That which the urine will not show.

"EXILES" A.E. RUSSELL (1867-1935)

The gods have taken alien shapes upon them,
Wild peasants driving swine
In a strange country. Through the swarthy faces
The starry faces shine.

Under grey, tattered skies, they strain and reel there:
Yet, cannot all disguise
The majesty and beauty of the fallen gods, the beauty,
The fire beneath their eyes.

They huddle at night within low, clay-built cabins;
And, to themselves unknown,
They carry with them a diadem and scepter
And move from throne to throne.

"IMMORTALITY" (A.E.)

We must pass like smoke or live within the spirit's fire,
For we can no more than smoke unto the flame return,
If our thought has changed to dream or will unto desire.
As smoke, we vanish though the fire might burn.

Lights of infinite pity star the grey dusk of our days:
Surely, there is the soul; with it, we have eternal breath:
In the fire of Love, we live or pass in many ways,
By unnumbered ways of dreaming to death.

"HAUNTED HOUSES"
HENRY WADSWORTH LONGFELLOW

_These perturbations, this perpetual jar
Of earthly wants and aspirations high,
Come from the influence of an unseen star,
An undiscovered planet in our sky.

And as the Moon from some dark gate of cloud
Throws over the sea a floating bridge of light,
Across whose trembling planks our fancies crowd
Into the realm of mystery and night,

So from the world of spirits, there descends
A bridge of light connecting it with this,
Over whose unsteady floor that sways and bends,
Wander our thoughts above the dark abyss.

"CHILDE HAROLD'S PILGRIMAGE" BYRON

Stars! Which are the poetry of heaven!
In your bright leaves, we would read the fate
Of men and empires. It's to be forgiven,
That in our aspirations to be great,
Our destinies overlap their mortal state,
And claim a kindred with you, for you are
A beauty and a mystery, and create
In us, such love, and reverence from afar,
That fortune, fame, power, life...
Have named themselves a star.

DJWHAL KHUL (THE TIBETAN)

Were all religions and scriptures of the world to be lost,
And were there nothing left to us except the starry heavens,
The story of the Zodiac and the significance of the names of
The various stars found in the different constellations,
We should be able to retrace the history of man,
Recover the knowledge of our goal and learn
The mode of its achievement.

SECRET WISDOM OF ANCIENT VERSES
PART TWO
"THE MAGIC OF THE MUSE"

THE GENTLEMAN'S MAGAZINE INTRODUCTION
(MR. SYLVANUS URBAN 1768)

Again, my friend Urban, as Time runs along,
And calls for your volume, I'll give him my Song.
He'll dispose of them stories where he may find them again,
And joined to your Book, he'll take care of my Strain.
But why, with a frown of Reproach, cries the Muse,
Degrade Father Time to a Hawker of News?
In Verse, you should rank him with Heroes and Kings,
For Time is the Regent of temporal Things;
From Vulgar Conceptions your Measures you've freed us;
Let Time be old Hercules, Urban Antaeus
Though Urban with Time has long ventured to strive,
He still is unconquered, alert, and alive:
At the End of each Month, on his Back though he lies,
He yields but to Triumph and falls but to Rise.
May you long, my friend Urban, continue the Fight,
The world shall applaud and look on with delight:
Some Advantage from Time we shall learn to secure,
His Threats to despise and his Blows to endure;
We shall learn if the Path that you point us we tread,
To live on when this hardy old Bruiser is dead

"ASTRONOMICA"
BY MANILIUS

BODY PARTS
BY CONSTELLATION'S:

The Ram [Aries], as the chief of them all, is allotted the head and
The Bull [Taurus] receives as of his estate the handsome neck;
Evenly bestowed, the arms to shoulders joined are accounted to The Twins [Gemini];
The breast is put down to The Crab [Cancer],

The realm of the sides and the shoulder blades with the heart are the Lion's [Leo],
The belly comes down to The Maid as her rightful lot [Virgo];
The Balance [Libra] governs the loins,
And Scorpion takes pleasure in the groin;
The thighs hie to The Centaur Archer [Sagittarius],
Capricorn is a tyrant of both knees,
While The Pouring Waterman [Aquarius] has the lordship of the shanks,
And over the feet, The Fishes [Pisces] claim jurisdiction.

In humankind's history, with so many wars, even for peace, loyal support is nowhere to be found. There's but one Pleiades but one Orestes, eager to die for his friend. How impossible to relieve Earth's hate. Loyalty bonds are rare and granted to few;

The RAM befriends his triangle of LEO and The ARCHER, but RAM respects more than the other two of their greed and ferocity, and gratitude from kindness will be short-lived.
The BULL is joined to CAPRICORN but with hard-to-blend temperaments.
The BULL embraces THE VIRGIN, but they often quarrel. The TWINS, the SCALE, and the WATERMAN are of one heart, with an indestructible loyalty bond. SCORPION and CRAB can become brothers and unite with the FISHES, but unstable like they come and go.

Opposite sign planets mostly hate. Square signs are for family ties. Friendships go to triagonal signs. The BULL has no real partner, nor the fierce LION; the mateless SCORPION has no one to fear, and The WATERMAN is a single sign too. Squares will unite us by marriage, and in kinship, they stamp children's features, and by the feelings of the heart, constellations conduct us to friendships that will rival blood ties.

VIRGO
BY MANILIUS

Modest Virgo's rays give polished parts,
And fill men's breasts with honesty and arts;
No tricks for gains, nor love for wealth dispense,
But piercing thoughts and winning eloquence.

HEBREW BIBLE, BOOK OF JOB

Who is this that darkens counsel by words without knowledge?
Where were you when I laid the foundations of the Earth? Declare it if you have the understanding.
Have the gates of death been revealed to you? Or have you seen the gates of the shadow of death?
Have you surveyed the breadth of the Earth? Declare it if you know it all.
Have you entered the treasuries of the snow, or have you seen the treasuries of the hail, which I have reserved against the time of trouble, against the day of battle and war?
Out of the Chamber comes the storm and cold out of the North.
By what way is the light parted, or the East wind scattered on the Earth?
Do you know the ordinances of heaven? Can you set their dominions on the Earth? Look up to the heavens, and see; and behold the skies, which are higher than you. Who commands the Sun, and it does not rise? Who seals up the stars?
Can you bind secure the sweet influences of the Pleiades or loose the bands of Orion? Can you lead forth Mazzaroth (skylights) in their season? Can you guide the Bear with it's children?
Who makes the Bear, Orion and the Pleiades and the chambers of the South? Who has put wisdom in the inward parts? Who gave understanding to the mind?

"THE PLANETARY FIVE"
BY WOODWORTH

... The planetary five,
With a submissive reverence, they beheld;
Watched from the centers of their sleeping flocks,
Those radiant Mercuries, that seemed to move,
Carrying through aether in the perpetual round,
Decrees and resolutions of the gods.

"THE PLANETS"
BY ISIDORE OF SEVILLE

The planets receive their spirit from the Sun,
Their bodies from the Moon,
Their intelligence and speech from Mercury,
Their pleasure from Venus,
Their blood from Mars,
Their disposition from Jupiter, and
Their bodily humors from Saturn.

"SIRENS" BY ISIDORE OF SEVILLE

The Greeks imagine three sirens, Part virgins, part birds,
With wings and claws,
One sang, one played the flute and the third with the lyre. They drew sailors to shipwreck by song.
But according to truth, they were prostitutes,
Leading travelers to poverty and imposing shipwreck on them. They had wings and claws because love flies and wounds; They stayed in the waves because a wave created Venus.

"THE SILENCE OF THE SIRENS" BY FRANZ KAFKA

Now, the sirens have a still more fatal weapon than their song,
Namely their silence. And through admittedly such a thing never happened,
It is still conceivable that someone might possibly have escaped from their
Singing, but not from their silence, certainly never.

"SIRENS" BY LEONARDO DA VINCI

The siren sings so sweetly that she lulls mariners to sleep, Then climbs upon their ships and kills the sleeping mariners.

"FEAR" BY HOMER

Feared you shall be 'Dear Father' and revered.
Bravery is not imagined, plain fearlessness to be
But a fear of disgrace and blame;
For those who are most timid to laws,
To enemies most boldness shows,
And those who are least afraid of danger
Are most afraid of just reproach.
Therefore, 'Reverence is still based on fear.'

"THE SEASONS, (COMETS)"
JAMES THOMSON (1930-1948)

From his huge vapouring train, perhaps to shake
Reviving moisture on the numerous orbs,
Throw which his long ellipsis winds, perhaps
To lend new fuel to declining suns,
To light up worlds and feed the ethereal fire

"PHYSICIAN OF SOULS OBSERVANCE"
BY EVAGRIUS (345-399AD)

Master your incensive powers
For 'He' will teach the gentle his ways.
Acts of mercy like medicine treats irascibility,
Prayer purges the soul; and
Fasting atrophies desire.
From these virtues, the New Man is formed,
Renewed to the image of his creator.'
In whom, thanks to holy apatheia,
becomes neither male nor female, and
Thanks to Faith and Love,
There is no Christian, Jew barbarian, bond man or free,
But Christ is all and in all.

"THE WORLD WERE FRAMED
BY THE WORD OF GOD" HEB.Xi.3

Mysterious night! When our first parent knew thee
From report divine, and heard thy name,
Did he not tremble for this lovely frame,
This glorious canopy of light and blue?
Yet, under a curtain of translucent dew,
Bathed in the rays of the great setting flame,
Hesperus, with all the hosts of heaven, came.

"THE MAGI"
BY WILLIAM BUTLER YEATS

Now, as at all times, I can see in the mind's eye,
In their stiff, painted clothes, the pail unsatisfied ones,
Appear and disappear in the blue depth of the sky;
With their ancient faces like rain-beaten stones, and
All their eyes still fixed, hoping to find again,
The uncontrollable mystery of the bestial floor.

MARIUS VICTOR (1599)

Diseases, famine, enemies, in us no change have brought;
Whatever we were we are, we were still in the same snare caught;
No time can our corrupted manners mend,
In vice we dwell, in sin that has no end, and
From then, our kind, hard heart is, enduring pain and care;
Proving that our bodies form a stony nature.

The Sun may set and rise, but we, contrariwise,
Sleep after our short light, one everlasting night.

SIR WALTER RALEIGH'S LAST WORDS BEFORE HIS EXECUTION

This home I draw, as death's long night draws on,
Yet, every foot, old thoughts turn back mine eyes;
Constraint me guides, as old age draws a stone
Against the hill, which over weighty lies

For feeble arms or wasted strength to move:
My steps are backward, gazing on my loss,
My mind's affection and my soul's sole Love,
Not mixed with fancy's chaff or fortune's dross.

To God, I leave it, who first gave it to me,
And I her gave, and she returned again,
As it was hers, so let His mercies be
Of my last comforts, the essential mean.

But be it so or not, the effects are past;
Her love hath end, my woe must ever last.

"SOLYMAN AND ALMENA"
JOHN LANGHORNE

Wealth corrupts man's heart with pride and complicates all good things in life.
Let the sons and daughters of Affliction receive comfort from Hope,
The motion of the sunbeam on the wave is no more uncertain than
The condition of human life: Where Misery has much to hope and
Happiness much to fear, but Virtue has always been a resource in Providence,
Improving the blessings and mitigating the evils of life.

"HYMN TO THE RISING SUN"

JOHN LANGHORNE

From the red wave rising bright,
Lift on high your golden head;
Over misty mountains spread
Your smiling rays of orient light.

See the golden God appear!
Flies the dreary darkness demon
Flies, and in her gloomy train,
Sable grief, care, and pain!

See the golden God advance!
On Taurus' heights, his courses prance:
With him haste the vernal hours,
Breathing sweets and dropping flowers.

Laughing summer at his side,
Waves her locks in rosy pride;
And autumn bland, with aspect kind,
Bears his golden sheaf behind.

O haste, and spread the purple day
Over all the wide ethereal way!
Nature mourns at your delay:
God of glory, haste away!

From the red wave rising bright,
Lift on high your golden head;
Over misty mountains spread
Your smiling rays of oriented light!

HERMES TRISMEGISTUS

That which is below corresponds to that which is above,
And that which is above corresponds to that which is below,
To accomplish the miracle of the one thing.

O son, how many bodies have we to pass through,
How many bands of demons,
Through how many repetitions of series and cycles of stars,
Before we hasten to the One alone?

"ON LUCRETIUS"
BY VIRGIL

Happy he who discovered the causes of things and has cast beneath his feet
All fears, unavoidable fate, and the doom of the devouring underworld.

"THE BOTANIC GARDEN, THE ECONOMY OF VEGETATION"

BY ERASMUS DARWIN (1731-1802) ENGLAND

Roll on, you Stars! Exult in youthful prime,
Marking with bright curves the printless steps of time;
Near and more near your beamy stars approach,
And lessening orbs on lessening orbs encroach;
Flowers of the sky! You, too, to age, must yield,
Frail as your silken sisters of the field!
Star after star from Heaven's high arch shall rush,
Suns sink on suns, and systems, systems crush,
Headlong, extinct, to one dark center fall,
And Death and Night and Chaos mingle all!
Till over wreck, emerging from the storm,
Immortal Nature lifts her changeful form,
Mounts from her funeral pyre on wings of flame,
And soars and shines, another and the same.

IV EZRA

Come, weigh me the weight of fire,
Or measure me the measure of the wind,
Or recall me on the day that is past.

LEONARDO DA VINCI

O Lord, at the price of effort, you give all.
O time, you that consume all things!
O envious age, you destroy and devoured with the hard teeth of years,
The Age as it flies and glides in secret well deceiving the one and the other.
I thought that I was learning how to live while I was really learning how to die.

NOT BY BREAD ALONE FROM THE UNIVERSITY PRESBYTERIAN

Man does not live by bread alone but by harmonious beauty, truth and goodness,
Work and recreation, affection and friendship, aspiration and worship.

Not by bread alone but by the splendor of the firmament at night,
The glory of heaven at dawn, the blending of colors at sunset.

Not by bread alone, but by the majesty of ocean breakers,
The shimmer of moonlight on a calm lake,
The exquisite patterns of snow crystals are the creation of artists.

Not by bread alone but by the fragrance of roses, the scent of orange blossoms,
The smell of new-mown hay, the clasp of a friend's hand,
The tenderness of a mother's kiss.

Not by bread alone but by the lyrics of poets, the wisdom of sages,
The holiness of saints, the biographies of great souls.

Not by bread alone, but by comradeship and high adventure, seeking and finding,
Serving and sharing, loving and being loved.

Man does not live by bread alone but by being faithful in prayer,
Responding to guidance of the Holy Spirit,

Finding and doing the loving will of God now and eternally.

MY SYMPHONY
BY WILLIAM ELLERY CHANNING

To live content with small means;
To seek elegance rather than luxury, and refinement instead of fashion; To
be worthy, not respectable, and wealthy, not rich;
To study hard, think quietly, talk gently, act frankly;
To listen to stars and birds, children and sages, with an open heart;
To bear all with cheer, and bravely wait for occasions, and never hurry. In
few words, to let the spiritual, unbidden and unconscious,
Grow up through the common. This is my symphony.

WHAT I LIVE FOR
BY GEORGE LINNAEUS BANKS

I live for those who love me, for those who know me true;
For the heaven that smiles above me, and awaits my spirit too;
For the cause that lacks assistance, for the wrong that needs resistance, For
the future in the distance, and the good that I can do.

"MY CREED"
BY EDGAR A. GUEST

To live as gently as I can;
To be no matter where, a man;
To take what comes of good or ill and cling to faith and honor still,
To do my best, and let that stand the record of my brain and hand;
And then, should failure come to me, still work and hope for victory.

To have no secret place wherein I stoop unseen to shame or sin;
To be the same when I'm alone as when my every deed is known;
To live undaunted, unafraid of any step that I have made;
To be without pretense or sham exactly what men think I am.

To leave some simple mark behind to keep my having lived in mind;
If enmity to aught I show, to be an honest, generous foe,
To play my little part, nor whine that greater honors are not mine.
This I believe, is all I need for my philosophy and my creed.

CHALLENGE
BY CARL D. ROLLINS

I marvel at the courage of the shrub or little tree
That struggles among rocks, well knowing it can never be Much more than
just a scrawny scrub, yet serving in God's plot To add a little beauty to a
useless barren spot.
I've seen them cling tenaciously to sides of rocky bluff, As if in pure
defiance of those elements so rough;
Or else to strive to justify audacity to choose
Such most unlikely habitat with odds so great to loose. They send their
eager tendons out along thin veins of soil, Extracting meager sustenance for
their persistent toil; Thus serving as a challenge to us mortals who complain
About the petty hardships that we often entertain.

BY UNKNOWN:
"PARADOX"

It is in loving_not in being loved,_the heart is blessed;
It is in giving not in seeking gifts, we find our quest.
If you are hungry, lacking heavenly food,_give hope and cheer.
If you are sad and need comfort_lift up someone.
Whatever is your longing and need, that you do give;
So that your soul be fed and you may truly live.

"MAY YOU HAVE"

Enough happiness to keep you sweet, Enough trials to keep you strong,
Enough sorrow to keep you human, Enough hope to keep you happy;
Enough failure to keep you humble, Enough success to keep you eager,
Enough friends to give you comfort, Enough resources to meet your needs;
Enough enthusiasm to look forward,
Enough faith to banish depression,
Enough determination to make everyday day better.

"REGRET'

I have wept in the night
For the shortness of sight
That to somebody's need I've been blind;
But I have never felt any regret for being just a bit too kind.

JOHN BANESTER TABB
"EVOLUTION"

Out of the dusk a shadow, then a spark;
Out of the cloud a silence, then a lark;
Out of the heart a rapture, then a pain;
Out of the dead, cold ashes, life again.

"THE CAPTIVES"

A part forever dwelt the two,
Safe for one often repeated strain,
Wherein what Love alone could say
They learned and lavished day by day.

Strangers in all but misery
And music's hope-sustaining tie,
They lived and loved and died apart,
But soul to soul and heart to heart.

DECEMBER

Dull sky above, dead leaves below;
Hungry winds that whining go.
Like faithful hounds upon the track
Of one beloved that comes not back.

LOVE'S AUTOGRAPH

Once only did he pass my way.
"When will you come again?
Ah, leave some token of your stay!"
 He wrote (and vanished) "Pain."

THE PORTRAIT

Each has his Angel-Guardian. Mine, I know,
Look on me from that pictured face. Behold,
How clear, between those rifted clouds of gold,
The radiant brow! it is the morning glow
Of innocence, here yet the heart lets go
The leading-strings of Heaven. Upon the eyes
No shadow: like the restful noonday skies
The sanctify the teeming world below.
Why bows my soul before it? None but you,
O tender child, has known the life estranged
From you and all that made your days of joy
The measure of my own. Behold me now_
The man that begs a blessing of the boy_
His very 'self' but from himself how changed!

"TRANSLATION"
BY JORGE SANTAYANA

Our knowledge is but faith moving in the dark,
Our joy a gift of grace,
Our immortality a subtle translation of time into eternity,
Where all that we have missed is ours and where what
We call ours is the least part of ourselves.
All belongs to the necessary passion and death of the spirit,
That today rides upon an ass into its kingdom, To be crucified tomorrow
between two thieves, And on the third day to rise again from dead.

JOHN MILTON

"SAMSON AGONISTES"

All is best, though we often doubt,
What the unsearchable dispose
Of highest wisdom brings,
And ever best found in the close.

"DEATH OF A FAIR INFANT DYING OF A COUGH"

O fairest flower no sooner blown but blasted,
Summer's chief honor if you had it outlasted,
Bleak Winter's force that made you blossom dry.
Yet I can't persuade me that you are dead
Or that your corpse corrupts in earth's dark womb,
Or that your beauty lies in wormy bed,
Hid from the world in a low delved tomb;
Could heaven for pity, you so strictly doom?
Oh no! for something in your face did shine
Above mortality that showed you were divine.
 But oh why did you not stay with us below
To bless us with you heaven's innocence,
To shake this wrath whom sin has made our foe
To turn swift-rushing black perdition here away,
Or drive away the slaughtering pestilence,
To stand between us and our deserved afflictions?
But you can best perform that office where you are.
Then you the mother of so sweet a child
Her false imagined loss cease to lament,
And wisely learn to curb you sorrows wild;
Think what a present you to God have sent,
And render him with patience what he lent;
This if you do he will an offspring give,
That till the world's last end shall make your name to live.

"HOW DO I LOVE YOU LET ME COUNT THE WAYS"
BY ELIZABETH BARRETT BROWNING

How do I Love you? Let me count the ways.
I Love you to the depth and breadth and height my soul can reach,
When feeling out of sight for the ends of Being and ideal Grace.
I Love you to the level of every day's most quiet need, by Sun and
candlelight.
I Love you freely, as men strive for Right;
I Love you purely, as they turn from Praise.
I Love you with the passion put to use,
In my old griefs, and with my childhood's faith.
*I Love you with a Love I seemed to lose,
With my lost saints, I Love you with the breath, smiles, tears, of all my life!
And, If God choose, I shall Love you better after death.

"NATURE"
BY HENRY WADSWORTH LONGFELLOW

As a fond mother, when the day is over,
Leads by the hand her little child to bed,
Half willing, half reluctant to be led,
And leave his broken playthings on the floor,
Still gazing at them through the open door,
Not wholly reassured and comforted
By promises of others in their stead,
Which, though more splendid, may not please him more;
So Nature deals with us, and takes away
Our playthings one by one, and by the hand
Leads us to rest so gently, that we go
 Scarce knowing if we wish to go or stay,
Being too full of sleep to understand
How far the unknown transcends the what we know.

"IMMORTALITY"
BY JOHN GREENLEAF WHITTIER

Yet Love will dream, and Faith will trust,
(Since he who knows our need is just)
That somehow, somewhere, meet we must.
For him who never sees,
The stars shine through his cypress trees!
Who, hopeless, lays his dead away,
Nor looks to see the breaking day
Across the mournful marble play!

Who has not learned, in hours of faith,
The truth to flesh and sense unknown,
That Life is ever Lord of Death,
And Love can never lose its own!

"MY COUNTRY"
BY BENJAMIN FRANKLIN

God grant me that not only the love of liberty
But a through knowledge of the rights of man
May pervade all nations of the Earth;
So that a philosopher may set his foot anywhere
On its surface, and say, "This is my country."

CELESTIAL MATH OF THEODORE ROOSEVELT

At night, I can look up and see the Spiral Galaxy of Andromeda. It is as large
as our Milky Way.
it's just one of a hundred million galaxies. It's 750,000 light years away.
It's made up of one hundred billion suns, Each of them larger than our
own.!
When I see myself small enough, then go to bed.

ANIMAL SUFFERING "VOICE OF THE VOICELESS"

I am the voice of the voiceless;
Through me the dumb shall speak,
Till the deaf world's ear be made to hear
The wrongs of the wordless weak.
From street, from cage, and from kennel,
From stable and zoo, the wail
Of my tortured kin proclaims the sin
Of the mighty against the frail.

"SOLITUDE"

Laugh and the world laughs with you,
Weep, and you weep alone;
The good old earth must borrow its mirth,
But has trouble enough of its own.

"THE GOAL"

All roads that lead to God are good;
What matters it, your faith or mine;
Both center at the goal divine
Of love's eternal brotherhood.

A thousand creeds have come and gone;
But what is that to you and me?
Creeds are but branches of a tree,
The root of love lives on and on.

Though branch by branch proves withered wood,
The root is warm with precious wine;
Then keep your faith, and leave me mine;
All roads that lead to God are good.

"THANKSGIVING"

We thank you for all the things that did not come to bother us,
For burdens we did not bear,
For troubles that passed us by,
For tasks we did not fail to do,
For hurts we did not keep;
For the friend who did not prove untrue,
For the joy that did not perish.
We give thanks for the blinding storm, that did not loose its swelling;
And for the sudden harm, that came not near our dwelling.
We thank you for unsent munitions,
And for the bitter word unspoken,
For lives remaining, for the tears not shed,
And for the heart ties that are still unbroken.

"MAKE A PEARL"
BY HARRY EMERSON FOSDICK

Most of us can take a lesson from the oyster.
When irritations gets in his shell that can't be rid off,
He settles down to make of them,
The loveliest thing the oyster has a chance to do:
It makes a pearl. It may even have to be a pearl of patience,
But anyhow, makes a pearl. And it takes faith and Love to do it.

ROBERT BROWNING HAMILTON
"PLEASURE AND SORROW"

I walked a mile with Pleasure, She chattered all the way,
But left me none the wiser For all she had to say.

I walked a mile with Sorrow, And she never said a word;
But, oh, the things I learned from her, When Sorrow walked with me!

"THE HUMAN SEASONS"

Four Seasons fill the Measure of the year;
Four Seasons are there in the mind of Man.
He has his lusty spring when fancy clear
Takes in all beauty with an easy span;
He has his Summer, when luxuriously
He chews the honied cud of fair spring thoughts,
Till, in his Soul dissolved they come to be
Part of himself. He has his Autumn ports
And Havens of repose, when his tired wings
Are folded up, and he content to look
On Mists in idleness: to let fair things
Pass by unheeded as threshold brook.

He has his Winter too of pale Misfeature,
Or else he would forget his mortal nature.

"DIGNITY OF MAN"
BY GIOVANNI PICO DELLA MIRANDOLA

The best Workman, decided to praise divine liberality and
He took man, a work of indeterminate form, and placing him at the
midpoint of The world, He spoke as follows:
Adam, you have been given no fixed seat,
No form of your own, no gift you may feel as yours.
You'll possess as your form, the gifts you desire.
A limited nature in other creatures is confined.
In your hands with free judgement I have placed you,
You are confined by no bounds, and yourself will fix limits of nature.
You have been placed in world's center, that from there you may see
What ever there is in the world.
Neither heavenly or earthly, neither mortal nor immortal you are.
You, as an Honorable judge are appointed, as your own molder and
maker; You can grow downward into the lower natures of beasts;
You can then again grow up from your soul's reason to higher natures,
Which are divine.
0 God the Father's great liberality!
0 great and wonderful happiness of man!
It is given him to have that which he's chosen, and to be that which he
wills.
When beasts are born, they bring with them from their dam's bag,
What they are going to possess.
Highest spirits have been, either from the beginning or soon after,
That which they are going to be throughout everlasting eternity.
At man's birth, in him the Father placed, every sort of seed and sprout
Of every kind of life.
The seeds each man grows and decides to cultivate,
Will grow and bear fruits inside him.
Cultivating vegetable seeds one becomes plant,
Cultivating seeds of sensation, he a beast shall become;
If rational, he will come out a heavenly animal;
If intellectual, he will come out an angel and a son of God.
And if he is not contented with the lot of any creature,
But takes himself up into center of his own unity, then,
Made one spirit with God and settled in the solitary darkness of:
The Father who is above all things, and will stand ahead of all things.

Who does not wonder at this chameleon which we are?
Or who feels more wonder at anything else whatsoever?
For it's not the rind which makes the plant, but a dull and non-sentient
nature;
Nor the hide which makes a beast of burden, but a brutal and sensual
soul;
Not the spherical body which makes the heavens, but right reason;
And not a separateness from the body but a spiritual intelligence that
makes an angel.
Wonderful man familiar with the upper and king of the lower;
Interpreter of nature and part in between the standstill of
Eternity and the flow of time, the bond tying the world together.

"THE EXTASIE"
BY JOHN DONNE

...Blood labors to beget Spirits as like souls as it can,
Because such fingers need to knit
The subtle knot that makes us man...

ABRAHAM COWLEY
"LIBERTY"

Would you be free? I'll show you friend the certain way:
By loosing things all others seek freedom is bought.
Who for fame and for riches aims, believe it, they a master need to take.

Freedom with virtue, her only place and scene is in the middle;
She lives not with the poor, nor with the great, the wings of those
Necessity has clipped, and they are in Fortune's bridewell whipped,
To the Laborious task of bread, these are by various tyrans captive led.
Now wild ambition with imperious force rides, and spurs like
a horse run wild. And sometimes lust, like the misguided light,
Draws them through all the labyrinth of night.
This very morning gladly I would yet sleep on,
But the stream of business does begin, those cruel guards
Which this poor prisoner do keep, that do not let me sleep;
And give me hours of liberty.
With a few friends that some relaxation give to mind,
To steal one day out of one's life to live.

In all the freedom nations of the air, never would a bird exchange his
liberty for soaring boldly up into the sky, freedom to sing, to perch, to
fly whenever he thought good,
And all innocent pleasures of the wood; for more plentiful and constant
food.
Nor ever could ambition bring him to a golden cage.
To keep the blessings of such heroic race, with all their powers and
rights so well (Though men and angels fell)

He is no small prince who every day can say: Now I sleep, now eat, now
sit, now walk,
Now meditate alone, now with acquaintance I will talk, this I will do,
here I will stay.
Where honor or conscience does not bind, will no other law enslave
myself.
Nor shall my future actions be confined for days that yet belong to Fate,
Like all received be always owed, not to enjoy but to pay debts.
For me serious will this matter be, with all the numbers loose and free,
It shall not keep on settled pace, in the same tune it shall not always
chime,
Nor shall each day just to his neighbor rhyme. A thousand liberties it
shall it dispense,
And try to manage all without offence, or greatness of the sense;
Like the Imperial Eagle will not stay till all what's fallen to it's power he
devours,

As if his generous hunger understood, that he can never plenty want of
food,
He only sucks the tasteful blood, and to fresh game flies cheerfully
away;
To kites and meaner birds he leaves the mangled prey for them to eat.

For the few hours of life assigned to me,
Give me great God, but Bread and Liberty.
I beg no more; if more you are pleased to give,
I'll thankfully that overplus receive.
If beyond this no more be freely sent,
I'll thank for this, and I content will go away.

"AMBITION"

Poverty wants some, luxury wants many, avarice wants all things.
Proportion well your cares to match the passage,
For it's a narrow string from start to end.
Don't let the Sun set on your greed or anger.
"As he would have more riches than his life could well contain,
"God destroyed his life and gave the fruits to someone else."
Sometimes this way will God takes us away from all our riches,
And with no less frequency will take away from us our riches.
Why heap up wealth, that we all must quit? Or worse, be left by it,
Why load yourself when you're to fly? 0 man, ordained to die.
Why build so high to later lie under the ground?
Be prudent and the shore in prospect keep,
In a weak boat trust not the deep.
From envy, place yourself beneath. Above everything rise;
Pity rich men, luxurious things despise.
Take as wise example, the heavenly lark,
Our fellow poet Cowley remarks:
"Above the clouds let your proud music sound,
Your humble nest build on the ground."
As far up towards heaven the branches grow,
So far the root sinks down to hell bellow.

"LIB 3 ODE 1"
BY HORACE

You, the Godless, I dislike you all, indecent great and small.
To decent minds not yet discolored with the love of gold, to you
The very few, these truths I'll tell, the muse inspires my song,
Listen and observe it well:
Beauty and strength, wit, wealth and power have their blooming but
short hour,
And love to see themselves and smile. Even so in the same land, poor
weeds,
Rich corn, gay flowers together stand to death's impartial mowing hand.
And all you men, whom greatness does so please but always with the
fear of Loosing things so near. If only your eyes would upwards move
(but you think Nothing is above) you would be able to perceive by what

a little thread
The sword still hangs above your head.
The man who in all wishes he does make, only Nature's counsel takes,
That wise and happy man will never fear the evil aspects of the year;
Nor tremble, though two comets should appear;
No need for almanacks to see, when Mars and Saturn in the heavens join,
And what they please against the world design, for so will Jupiter within him shine.
If men to their pleasures and desires can find no end.
God to their cares and fears will set no bounds.

"EVEN SUCH IS TIME" SIR WALTER RALEIGH

Even such is Time, that takes on trust
Our youth, our joys, our all we have,
And pays us but with earth and dust;
Who, in the dark and silent grave,
When we have wandered all our ways,
Shuts up the story of our days;
But from this earth, this grave, this dust
My God shall raise me up, I trust!

"IN DEFIANCE OF FORTUNE"

Never think 'Fortune' can bear the sway,
Where virtue's force can cause her to obey.

"ON MONSIEUR'S DEPARTURE"

I grieve and dare not show my discontent;
I love and yet I seem to hate;
I do, yet dare not say I ever meant;
I seem stark mute, but inwardly overtalk;
I am, and not; I freeze yet I am burned,
Since from myself another self I turned.

My care is like my shadow in the Sun
Follows me flying, flies when I pursue it,
Stands, and lies by me, does what I have done;
No means I find to rid him of my breast,
Till by the end things it be suppressed.

Some gentler passion stride into my mind,
For I am soft, and made of melting snow;
Love be so kind, or be more cruel
Let me or float or sink, be high or low;
Let me live with some more sweet content,
Or die, and so forget what loving ever meant.

"DEATH" BY SIR THOMAS MORE

Though I be foul, ugly, lean and misshape, Yet there is none in all this
worldwide, That may my power defy or escape; Therefore sage father,
greatly magnified,
Descend from your chair, set apart your pride, Vouch safe to lend,
though it be to your pain, To me, a fool, some of your wise brain.

'THE PSALMS OF THE SWEET SINGER'
BY FULKE GREVILLE (LORD BROOKE)

The Mind of Man is this world's true dimension;
And knowledge Is the measure of the Mind.
Mind's vast comprehension contains more worlds than all the World
can find:
So knowledge extends far more than all the minds of men can
comprehend;
A climbing height without a head; depth without bottom, way without
an end.
Not comprehending, all it comprehends; with infinite, it satisfies no
mind,
Till it that infinite of the Godhead finds.

'RING OF LIGHT' FOR ETERNITY
BY HENRY VAUGHAN

"The last chief oracle of what man knows is understanding,
Which thought contains some ruinous notion, which to our Nature
shows,
Of general truths, yet stained from our corruption, all light they loose:
Save to convince of ignorance and sin,
Which where they rule, they'll let no perfection in.
So few and weak are all the notions, that our understanding can retain.
..As man is bankrupt, Nature isn't free by arts to raise itself again,
To give those confused notions a well art-like state.
Nor in a right line can her eyes ascend, to view the things that
immaterial are;
For as the Sun does when the Sun's beams descend, 'to light the Earth,
but to Shadow every star.'
So Reason stooping to attend the sense, darkens the spirit's clear
intelligence."

SHAKESPEARE STANZAS

Those words must sparks be of those fires that they strike.
Some seek knowledge to be known, idle curiosity that is;
Some but to sell, not freely to bestow; these gain and spend both time
and wealth, Some build others, which is charity; but wise men are these
that build themselves.

As Godless wisdoms worthless are; His heights our true philosophy.
Which with fair cautions, man may well profess to study God,
Whom he is born to serve; Nature to admire the greater in the less;
Time, but to learn; ourselves we may obscure.

METAMORPHOSES
BY OVID (43BC-17AC)

If it's truth you want, read Holy scriptures.
In twice three days The Maker completed miracles which our eyes
behold even today. Out of nothing, He produced all things; and by it He
sustains all things he made. Creation was sorted out, the lightest bodies,
fiery aether, and below this, cold air, and all heavenly bodies claimed
the higher parts, the cosmos, the zone of Sun's splendor and Heavenly
Light, but the heaviest, namely earth and water, are situated in the
lowest part of all. With elements assigned and divided man was created
to be lord of Earth. Heaven then glittered with stars, birds coursed the
clear sky, bright Earth bore beasts and other brute creatures and there
emerged 'man' with a body of earth and immortal mind, Sacred will, and
a raised face that he might ever view heaven. Facing up the stars, our
hearts will be longing for heaven. Man has no fixed dwelling on Earth, so
he may seek his home above. True men aim ever high, fools hope for
secure seats down on Earth with goods that are short lived. "You!
Whoever you may be, always set your eternal aim above, the hour of
death robs. Ah! Our fated end knocks even now.
First, forbid to pollute yourselves with slaughtered creatures, for the
fields smile with corn, ripe fruit, plump grapes, their vines attire; there
are sweet herbs, and savory roots, milk, sweet honey, flowers of Thyme,
for your palate to content, the prodigal Earth abounds with gentle food,
affording banquets without death or blood. Brute beasts with flesh their
ravenous hunger cloy; and yet not all in pasture's Horses joy; so flocks
and herds, but those whose Nature has endowed with cruelty, and
salvage wrath, in hot blood delight. How horrible a sin, That entrails
bleeding entrails should in tomb! That greedy flesh, should fat become!
While by one creature's death another lives! Of all Earth mother gives;
can nothing please unless your teeth sink into wounds? Can
nothing satiate except the luxury that another dies? The Golden Age,
when Fowl through air, their wings in safety played; Hares fearless
wandered over plains, no Fish by their credulity were obtained. He who
crammed his guts with flesh, set open gates to cruel crimes. Audacious
first sacrifice, the Bore was thought to merit death who bladed corn.
You sheep, what ill did you? Such gentle beast, born to invest exposed
man with your soft wool and are alive then dead, a more profitable fare.

What the Ox, a creature without guile, so innocent, so simple born to work, he most ungrateful is, deserving ill, the gift of corn that can unyoke, then kill his painful! hind; that neck with axe to wound in service, that had the stubborn ground so often worked and many crops brought in to have the knife sheared with his blood. From where springs such appetite in man? 0 mortals! How can or dare you feed on flesh? To this words give ears when slaughtered beef becomes your meat, think and know that you your servants eat. Erring men that way unfold the book of fate.

VENUS
BY OVID

Venus from her mountain throne, saw Hades and clasped her swift-winged son, and said: 'Cupid, my child, my warrior, my power, take those sure shafts with which you conquer all, and shoot your arrows to the heart of the one to whom the last lot fell when the three realms were drawn. Your mastery subdues the gods of heaven, the ocean's deities and even Jove. Why should Hell lag behind? Why not there too? Extend your mother's empire and your own..
Then Cupid guided by his mother, opened up his quiver of all his thousand arrows, selected one, the sharpest and surest, the arrow most obedient to the bow, and bent the pliant horn against his knee and shot the barbed shaft deep in Pluto's heart.

I have finished the work, which neither the wrath of Jove, nor fire, nor the sword, nor devouring age shall be able to destroy.

NATURE
BY LUCRETIUS (99BC-55BC)

The human race forever works in vain,
Forever wasting time on empty worries,
The brief capacity of pleasure only for increase;
Ever slowly bringing lives to tidal depths and stormy wars.
Our terrors and our darkest minds must be dispelled,
Not by sunshine's rays but by studying Nature
And the ways she works;
A Nature that creates, maintains and multiplies,

The purpose of the skies the law behind,
The wandering courses of the Sun and Moon,
To scan the powers that speed all life below,
And most of all to see with reason's eyes:
Of what the mind and soul are made;
Until we seem to mark and hear at hand dead men,
Whose bones earth blossomed long ago.

CICERO (1068C-43BC) ROME

Just as the soul fills the body, so God fills the world.
Just as the soul bears the body, so God endures the world.
Just as the soul sees but is not seen, so God sees but is not seen. Just as
the soul feeds the body, so God gives food to the world.
As from a fire aflame, a thousand sparks come forth,
So from the Creator an infinity of beings have life and to him return.

ST AUGUSTINE

Men go abroad to admire, the heights of mountains,
The mighty waves of the sea, the broad tides of rivers,
The compass of the ocean and the circuits of stars;
Yet pass by the mystery of themselves without thought.

ST. FRANIS OF ASSISI (1181-1226)

Lord make me an instrument of your peace.
Where there is injury, pardon;
Where there is doubt, faith;
Where there is despair, hope;
Where there is darkness, light;
And where there is sadness, joy.
O divine Master,
Grant that I may not so much seek consolation as to console;
To be understood as to understand;
To be loved as to love;
For it's in giving that we receive;
It's in pardoning that we are pardoned;
And it's in dying that we are born.

Praise you my Lord, for all your creatures,
Above all brother Sun;
Who brings us the day and lends us his light,
And with radiant splendor shows us Thee, O most high.

PETRARCH (FRANCESCO DI PETRACCO)
ITALY 1304-1374CE

Friend, as we both in confidence complain
 To see our ill-hopes return in vain,
Let that chief good which must forever please,
Exalt out thoughts and renew our happiness.
This world as some gay flower field is spread,
Which hides a serpent in its painted bed,
And most it wounds when most it charms our eyes,
At once the tempter and the paradise.
Would you then sweet peace of mind restore,
And in fair calm expect your parting hour?
Leave the crowds and seek the happy few!
All to well may friend reply:

O Friend, you show others the same path,
From which you've so often strayed.

SIRIUS
BY E.W. WILCOX

Since Sirius crossed the Milky Way
Full sixty-thousand years have gone.
Yet hour by hour and day by day
This tireless star speeds on and on.

I think he must be moved to smile
By that amusing tale of Genesis,
Which says Creation had its birth
For such a tiny world as this.

To hear that One who fashioned all

Those solar systems tier on tiers,
Expressed in little Adam's fall
The purpose of a million spheres!

On planets old, before form or place
Was lent to Earth, may dwell, who knows?
A godlike and perfect race
That hails great Sirius as he goes.

VLADIMIR SOLOVYOV
(RUSSIA 1853-1900)

Again my tired lantern is lit up,
How it torches my eyes.
Dear God if I am a slave,
If I am weak and lack,
If I am to be tormented here forever,
Laboring just for songs.
Let me just for one night
My weakness overcome,
And with one completed creation
Pure for centuries, catch fire.

AMONG WORLDS
BY INNOKENTYANNENSKY (RUSSIA 1855-1909)

Among worlds flickering and shining,
A single star whose name I repeat..
Not so that I come to worship it
But because I am weary of the rest.
And If I find doubt a burden
Only from her I seek answers
Not because she shines so brightly
But because with her I need no light.

JOHANN WOLFGANG VON GOETHE-GERMANY (1749-1832)

It's hard to gather up assistance
Whereby one rises to the source!
The better soul awakes to light.
The wild desire no longer wins,
The deeds of passion cease to chain;
The love for Man revives within,
The love of God revives again.
Reason and Knowledge,
The highest strength in man there lies!
Then Hope again lends sweet assistance,
And Reason then resumes her speech:
One yearns, the rivers of existence,
To reach the very founts of Life.
Once I blazed across the sky, Leaving trails of flame;
I fell to Earth, and here I lie-
Who'll help me up again?
-A Shooting Star. Life is sweeping by
Go and dare before you die.
Something mighty and sublime,
To leave behind and conquer time.

ALEXANDER POPE
(ENGLAND 1688-1744)

Blind to former as to future fate,
What man knows his preexistent state?
A part we see and not a whole,
Extremes in nature equal ends produce;
In man they join to some mysterious use.
All are but parts of one stupendous whole,
Whose body Nature is, and God the soul.
Know then yourself, presume not God to scan,
The proper study for mankind is man.
One science only will one genius fit,
So vast the art, so narrow human wit.

Slave to no sect, take no private road,
But look through Nature up to Nature's God.

All things are bound with the indissoluble bonds of Necessity (which we call Fate) But when the better parts of the soul energize, the soul is then intimately Converted to itself, and through this conversion elevated to superior natures.

BLOOMFIELD'S BLOSSOMS
BY ISAAC NEWTON

Father Time set me at the gate
And delivered me a key to enter there.
'Unlock this Gate now by yourself' said he,
But I said one key could not all twelve locks unlock
Father Time replied,
'Open the first lock and you have opened all'
What's the first Lock name? I said
It's called the secret of all wise men
I proved every way and at last I did unlock
The crafty Gwynns thus made for the nonce
Other Locks fell open all at once
In the entry a number of Philosophers I met
Among them Hermes, Democritus, Albert Bacon & Ramund,
The Monk and Channon of Bridlington profound.
Ramund brought me to a garden green
And showed springing of a tree, and buds fifteen more
Of which Tree produce what we desire
The blessed stone one in number and no more
Who attains this treasure can never fade away
I leave you here now our secrets to attain.
Lift up the head and look upon the heaven
To know the Planets seven

B. VALENTINE'S MYSTERY OF THE MICROCOSM
BY ISAAC NEWTON

Bright glorious king of this world O Sun,
Whose progeny's upholder is the Moon,
Whom Priest Mercury does firmly bind,
Unless Dame Venus favor you do find,
Who for her spouse Heroic Mars has tamed,
Without her aid what here you do it's in vain.
Jove's grace do not neglect. Saturn old and gray,
In various hews will them display
From black to white, from white again to red
Mounting on stilts he'll walk till he be dead.
Returning into life again, in quiet rest he shall remain
Lady in greens cry, oh my son come
Antimony and assist me here.
Noble salt, come guard me and defend,
That worms of me make not an awful end.
 If all these things you can fit right,
In the last judgement they will delight.

HIGHEST PLANET SATURN

I am hugely melancholic
Saturday my day became
And It was from me it took it's name
My course is circular and finished every thirtieth year
Add six hours and five days.
Capricorn and Aquarius to me are both obnoxious
A beautiful Granat clear and brave
My Angel Oriphiel gave to me. My art's Astronomy,
My colors black, white, yellow, red will find.
My spirit's sweet, and cold as Ice.
For theft I bear away the price
But when my spirit's fettered,
I make good my promise.
I can tame and change and bind,
All else must be left behind.

Consider well and take good heed,
For I am not the common Lead.
Who bides with me shall want no blows
To unfixed metals I'm a deadly foe
And bring them all to anguish
But he who duly seeks and rightly knows
Has goods enough till death his eyes shall close
I cut and mow all down
And parting say unto the world mow now.

PLANET JUPITER

Thursday above all days is celebrated to my praise.
Zachariel is my Angel's name,
My subjects are Bowman and Fish,
To rich and poor I justice do
My tongue in rhetoric excels
When with Laurel leaves she crowned my head,
With roses all around, adding a golden crown,
Set with a glorious Topaz stone.
My colors are yellow, blue and white,
My journey I perform in haste,
In twelve years my whole course is past
Who's known in regions far and wide
May find my wealth in England hid.

PLANET MARS

With my sharp pointed steel
Many fights I run into.
The soldiers all put me in charge
To be their General!.
Samael is my Angel dear,
Had he not of me taken care
Since long I would be dead.
Although Ram and Scorpion
In wars owe me subjection,
Yet in the army some scurvy tricks
To me they played.

In peace I'm in a musty mood,
My virtue's name is Fortitude.
If I should chance to die the death,
Then all my goods I will bequeath
To Venus my high bread Queen,
Which afterwards she may present
According to her heart's content.
In two years I complete my course,
Which must to end be fully brought.
On Tuesday I declare my might,
Which many men esteem but light.

FROM ISAAC NEWTON'S PAPERS AT THE END OF MICROCOSM

Sol Lune & Mars with *Jove* (Jupiter) a hunting ride. And Saturn carries all the nets this tide:
Just in the round is placed Mercury, And so is caught Venus's Progeny.
Venus, a hunting hare you now do see
But if a hound should catch a hare then she Nere will much older grow affirm I dare whereof Don Mercury is well aware.
For Venus, once beginning to grow proud
Makes many hares grow monstrous fierce & word wherefore o Mars draw out thy killing sword
That thy much loved Venus be not whoor'd.

HADRIAN
(ROME 76-138)

O blithe little soul, you, flitting away,
Guest and comrade of this my clay,
Whither now goest thou, to what place
Bare and ghastly and without grace?
Nor, as thy wont was, joke and play.

Blissful little soul, you're flying away,
My clay body's Guest and comrade.
Where do you go, to what place
Bare and frightful and without grace?

Not in the way you liked to joke and play.

THE CRAFTS OF OLDEN TIME
BY FREEMASON W. SNEWING

All honor to our forefathers, the Craftsmen true of old;
Propounders of the sacred truths which we their children hold,
 And guard with jealous caution, as the miser would his gold,
Safe from the coward's crafty wile, and him who battles hold,
As did our ancient Brethren, the Craft of olden time.

It was their to rear the stately dome, aspiring to the skies,
While wondering crowds astonished viewed, the stately structure rise;
And deemed the labor magic, in their wonder and surprise;
Nor know that science in our hand, a giant's strength supplies,
Well known unto our forefathers, the Crafts of olden time.

Nor were their useful labors to brick and stone confined;
I was theirs to mold in beauty's form the rude unpolished mind,
Which, by their moral regime, exalted and refined,
Fulfilled the noble destiny for which it was designed.
Thus wrought our ancient Brethren, the Crafts of olden time.

Our ancient Brethren emulous, in virtue took delight;
And zealously and fervently, contented for 'the right'_
Not with the arm of earthly power or sword of carnal might;
But with the spear of Reason" and the Force of moral light.
Thus strove our ancient Brethren, the Crafts of olden time.

Each atom of creation, which met the curious eye,
From earth's light dust, unto the orbs which stud the azure sky,
Was listed in the noble work, and made to magnify,
The Wisdom of the Great 'I am'_ the power of the Most High.
So pious were our Brethren, the Crafts of olden time.

Then let us strive to emulate, those virtues which have made,
The name of Mason glorious, as Sol in light arrayed;
And demonstrate to all the earth, that ages have conveyed
Undimmed to us the holy 'Light' whose guiding luster swayed

The action of our Brethren, the Crafts of olden time.

'SYMPATHISE'
FROM THE FREEMASON'S MAGAZINE VOL.S-6

Ah, who can tell how many a soul sublime,
Has felt the influence of malignant star,
And waged with fortune an eternal war,
Checked by the scoff of Pride, by Envy's frown
And Poverty's unconquerable bar,
In life's low vale remote, has pined alone,
Then dropped into the grave unpitied and unknown.

THE SILENT LOVER
BY SIR WALTER RALEIGH TO QUEEN ELIZABETH

Passions are like floods and streams,
The shallow murmur, but the deep are dumb,
So when affections yield discourse,
It seems the bottom is shallow where they come.
'They, that are rich in words,
In words discover that they are poor
In that which makes a lover.
Sweet express think not, that he feels no smart,
That sues for no compassion,
Since lack of conquest of your beauty,
Comes not from defect of love
But from excess of duty.

DAVISON'S POETICAL RAPSODY (1602-1621)

Infatuation by the eyes,
It's quickly born and quickly dies,
For while reason makes his grave;
For many things the eyes approve,
Which the heart is seldom yet to love;
For as the seeds in spring time sown,
Die in the ground before they grow,
So infatuation whose rooting fails,
As a child within the mother's womb
Has his beginning and his end.
Affection follows torture's wheels.
As soon as shaken from his heels;
For following beauty or fortune,
The liking soon is turned to hate,
For all affections have their change,
And fancy only loves to range.
Desire himself runs out of breath,
And getting does but gain his death.

STARS
BY GOETHE

Though still by them uncomprehended,
From these the angels draw their power,
And all Thy works, sublime and splendid,
Are bright as in Creation's hour.

STARS
BY ERASMUS DARWIN

Roll on, you stars! Exult in youthful prime,
Mark with bright curves the printless steps of time;
Near and more near your beamy cars approach,
And lessening orbs on lessening orbs enroach.

STARS
BY BYRON

You stars! Which are the poetry of heaven!
A beauty and a mystery, and create
In us such love and reverence from far
That fortune, fame, power, life, have named themselves a star.

HENRY VAUGHAN (1622-1695)

I saw Eternity the other night
Like a great ring of pure and endless light.
All calm, as it was bright;
And round beneath it,
Time in hours, days, years, driven by the Spheres.

Some men a forward motion love,
But I, by backward step would move.

Death, the jewel of The Just! Shinning only in the dark;
What mysteries do lie beyond your dust.

DANTE ALIGHIERI (1265-1321)

As I'd journeyed half my life away
I found I'd lost the path that does not stray;
I looked on and high, by the rays of that same planet
Which serves to lead men straight along all roads.

I learned that love moves the Sun and stars,
O human race, born to fly up,   ·
Yet, with little wind you fall.

Pride, Envy, Avarice
Are the three sparks
That have set hearts on fire.

You will prove how hard
Is the way up and down
Another man's stairs.
The experience of this sweet life!

The sight granted to the world,
 Penetrates within the Eternal Justice
As the eye penetrates into the sea:
From the shore it sees bottom,
In the open sea, the depth's concealed.

PLATO (GREECE 429-347 BCE) ASTER(STAR

The Morning Star, Aster, vibrant and alive
You shone with brilliant light;
And now you glow among the dead,
The Star that heralds night.

MENANDER (GREECE 344-292 BCE)

Fate steers, fate governs, fate might preserve;
Each thought by chance, each word and act by chance, All human
forethought can turn to smoke,
All men can do is sign the dotted line.

FURIES BY AESCHYLUS (GREECE 525-456 BC)

Destiny!
Without beginning, without an end,
We Furies, to fate's decree abide;
Immortal Angels are white, We are black
Destruction is ours.
We hunt men down,
The men who killed and knew they killed,
Beneath the earth
In the underwood they learn
That from us,
Not even the dead are free.
The fool, he falls
Who knows not his fall,
With pride,
Man thinks himself above
Our voices whisper in the dark,
We stalk,
Run as he may, we bring him down;
Vengeance pulsing is our dance
 Our task is fixed,
Forever fixed, forever true.
Do evil and we remember,
Deaf to all appeal
Under a black sun Despised, we do our work
Fear our ancient powers mortal man!
In sunless slime
We live the haunts of darkness.

PYRAMID TEXTS 284, 523

"A stairway to the sky is set up for me that I may ascend to the sky..."
"May the sky make the sunlight strong for you, may you rise up to the sky"

HAFEZ-E SIRAZI (PERSIA 1325-1389)

Even after all this time,
The Sun never says to the Earth:
"You owe me"
Look what happens with a love like that,
It lights up the whole sky.

KHALIL GIBRAN (LEBANON 1883-1931)

I am alive like you, and I am standing beside you. Close your eyes and
look around, You will see me in front of you. You are my brother and I
love you. I love you when you prostrate yourself in your mosque, and in
your church and pray in your synagogue. You and I are sons of one faith,
the Spirit, for the diverse paths of religion are fingers of the loving hand
of God, extended to all. O Living Jesus, return to chase the merchants of
faith out of your sacred temple. Kindness should be the source of every
law upon the earth, for kindness is the shadow of God in man. Your
children are not your children, they are the songs and daughters of life's
longing for itself.
Half of what I say is meaningless, but I say it so that the other half will
reach you.

LOVE

When love beckons to you follow him.
Though his ways are hard and steep.
When his wings enfold you, yield to him.
When he speaks to you believe in him.
Though the sword hidden may wound you,
And his words may shatter your dreams,
As the North wind lays waste the garden.
For even as love crowns you so shall he crucify you.
Even as he ascends to your height
And caresses your tender branches that quiver in the Sun,
So shall he descend to your roots and shake them in their clinging to the earth.
Love will knead you till you're pliant;
Love grinds you to whiteness.
And then assigns you to his sacred fire,
That you may become sacred bread for God's sacred feast.
But if in your fear you seek only love's peace and pleasure,
Then it's better that you cover your nakedness
And pass out of love's threshing floor,
Into the seasonless world, where you shall laugh,
But not all your laughter, and weep, but not all of your tears.
Love gives nothing but itself and takes nothing but from itself.
Love possesses and will not be possessed;
For love is sufficient to love.
When you love, you're in God's heart.
Don't think you can direct love's course,
For love if it finds you worthy will direct your course.
If you love, melt like a running brook that sings its melody to the night.

THE FAREWELL

What is to die but to stand naked in the wind and to melt into the Sun?
Now I'm ready, fare well,
This day has ended.
Don't forget I shall comeback to you.
A little while, a moment of rest upon the wind,
And another woman shall bear me.
Farewell to you and the youth I have spent with you.
It was but yesterday we met in a dream.
It's no longer Dawn, the Noontide is upon us and we must part.
In the twilight of memory we should meet again.
And if our hands should meet in another dream,
We shall build another tower in the sky.
A little while, a moment of rest upon the wind,
And another woman shall bear me.

EATING AND DRINKING

If only you could live on the fragrance of the earth, and like an air plant
be sustained by the light; but if you must kill to eat, and rob the young
of its mother's milk to quench your thirst, let it be an act of worship:
When a beast is killed to feed you, say to him in your heart,
"By the same power that slays you, I too am slain; and I too shall be
consumed. For the law that delivered you to me shall deliver me into a
mightier hand.
Your blood and my blood is but the sap that feeds the tree of heaven."
When you crush an apple with your teeth, say to it in your heart:
"Your seeds shall live in my body,
And the buds of your tomorrow shall blossom in my heart, And your
fragrance shall be my breath,
And together we shall rejoice through all seasons."
And in the autumn, when the grapes are gathered for the winepress,
say in your heart: "I too am a vineyard, and my fruit shall be gathered
for the winepress,
And like new wine I shall be kept in eternal vessels."
And in winter, when you drink the wine let there be in your heart a song
for each cup, and with the song remember the autumn days and the
vineyard.

BLEND

Love is the only gold, it wakes up the soul. Love is the only bow on life's dark cloud,
It is the morning and the evening star, It shines upon the cradle of the babe,
And sheds it's radiance upon the quiet tomb. Only one life, that soon is past,
Only what's done with love will last.
I feel love when I sorrow most, It's better to have loved and lost, Than never to have loved at all.
Love is calm, and is shown with deeds.
Love never dies. Love makes things worthwhile.
Loved you then, love you still, always have, always will.

William Fish bough 1852

Nature is a Harp of seven times seven strings, On which, by God's own hand, is gently played The ever varied music of the Spheres.

CHILDREN OF THE GODS. A.B. Curtiss

Division, everywhere contradiction;
One can count on nothing. And for what? To learn the hurt of loss,
the joy of gain, to try and fail, succeed, yet win in vain.
For no sooner will we get our heart's desire, then we'll find it is
another empty cup we need to fill; and all we have is at great cost.
With no burden but excess desire, no sin but excess busyness.
Divided from the center, nothing works except the middle.
What seems like opportunities, turn out into entrapments to
betray ourselves once more. What do we do?
The next thing, there is always a next thing. And nothing comes again.

UNKNOWN

Our lives through various scenes are drawn,
And vexed with trivial cares,
While our eternal thought moves on,
Our undisturbed affairs.

PICI MIRANDOLA

As an architect has in his mind a figure
Of the building he undertakes,
Which as his pattern he exactly strives to imitate,
So none any work can frame,
Unless himself becomes the same.
God producing intelligible mind,
Then produced all.

EOLAUS by James Allen

O Solitude! habitation of aspiring hearts,
Teacher of the teachable and true.
Sorrow darkens all the Universe;
It's creatures are involved in pain,
Helpless, no one hears or aids;
Life is dark, none it's meaning know,
In the hospital of Earth, Arise!
shake off the dreams of night,
See the light, leave the fleeting shapes of time,
No fear, no grief, no lust; scorn the self whose end is dust.
Knowledge is for him who seeks,
Peace in sinless silence speaks;
All things perish, truth survives.
Be no slave of lusts and cravings;
A little fever of delights, torn away, not to endure.
Life is passing, while it seems to wait, what grows decays,
What rises falls, what flourishes does fade away.
There is no rest in life nor death, In truth is rest.
The law of laws is in thy mind,
And written in the tablet of thy heart.
Truth in passion is preserved,
But not known till passion be destroyed, and cast away.
Who can see the Cosmos and be sad?
Who seeks to stand must fall,
Ascending to the high, must know the low.
Who would know the great,
Must not disdain to wait upon the small.
Wisdom finds humility. Truth finds self-control.
Holy Ones know not the name of sin,
All things are holy to the holy mind.
Let praise, reward, and popularity be sweet no more. Pure thoughts,
selfless deeds,
Until the edifice of truth there rises and appears.
At last, I see the path of peace; the lowly way will enter in.
Evil, is good denied.
Be watchful, fearless, faithful, patient, pure.

Look the passion tortured multitudes,
Know their pain and have compassion.
I am the sunshine and the storm,
The creeping action that deceives,
The lie, the theft, the murderer's ire,
All burn in my celestial fire.
All that debases and defiles, I grind and in the dust I scatter.
Nations rise, empires fall,
The drama of the Universe; I all their fleeting forms enfold.
Who has my vision finds release,
From darkness and captivity.
I am. Perfection is. And peace.

9 781965 190883